ANTEBELLUM CHARLESTON
DRAMATISTS

INDEPENDENCE,

OR

WHICH DO YOU LIKE BEST,

THE

PEER, OR THE FARMER?

A COMEDY,

IN FIVE ACTS.

(FOUNDED ON THE NOVEL OF " THE INDEPENDENT,")

AND PERFORMED AT THE THEATRE, CHARLESTON,

WITH UNBOUNDED APPLAUSE.

BY WILLIAM IOOR,

OF ST. GEORGE, DORCHESTER, SOUTH-CAROLINA.

" Oh knew he but his happiness, of men
" The happiest he! who, far from public rage,
" Deep in the vale, with a choice few retir'd,
" Drinks the pure pleasures of a country life."　THOMPSON.

CHARLESTON:

PRINTED FOR THE AUTHOR,

BY G. M. BOUNETHEAU, NO. 3, BROAD-STREET.

[Price one Dollar.]

M,DCCCV.

TITLE PAGE OF WILLIAM IOOR'S FIRST PLAY.
COURTESY, EMMETT ROBINSON

Antebellum Charleston Dramatists

CHARLES S. WATSON

THE UNIVERSITY OF ALABAMA PRESS
University, Alabama

To my mother
EMILY SULLIVAN WATSON

Publication of this book
was assisted by a grant from the
South Carolina Historical Society

Copyright © 1976 by
THE UNIVERSITY OF ALABAMA PRESS

Library of Congress Cataloging in Publication Data:
Watson, Charles S. 1931–
Antebellum Charleston Dramatists.
Bibliography: p.
Includes index.
1. American drama—Charleston, S.C.—History and criticism. 2. American drama—19th century—History and criticism. 3. Theater—Charleston, S.C.—History. I. Title.
PS343.W3   812'.3'09   75–30635
ISNB 0–8173–6001–8

CONTENTS

ACKNOWLEDGMENTS

I wish to express my gratitude to the following persons for their assistance and encouragement in the making of this book: Thomas Daniel Young and Herschel Gower of Vanderbilt University; Elizabeth McDavid of Pelzer, South Carolina; W. Stanley Hoole, Dean Emeritus of University Libraries, The University of Alabama; Joy Crosson, for typing the manuscript; Mrs. Billy Hart of Summerville, South Carolina; and my wife, Juanita Goodman Watson. In Charleston I am happy to acknowledge the kind help of Mary B. Prior, director of the South Carolina Historical Society, Dr. Joseph Ioor Waring, Joseph H. McGee, the late Helen McCormack, Emmett Robinson, Virginia Rugheimer, and the staffs of the Charleston Library Society and the South Carolina Historical Society. For a grant to assist in publication of this book I am grateful to the South Carolina Historical Society. For permission to quote from letters thanks are due the South Carolina Historical Society and the Historical Society of Pennsylvania. For permission to use material from three of my published articles, I wish to thank *Louisiana History* and the *South Carolina Historical Magazine*. I also wish to express my appreciation to the staff of The University of Alabama Library and to The University of Alabama Research Grants Committee for two grants. Other institutions to which I am indebted are the Southern Historical Collection of The University of North Carolina Library, the University of Pennsylvania Library, the Massachusetts Historical Society, and the South Caroliniana Library. My appreciation is especially due to Walter J. Meserve of Indiana University and George C. Rogers, Jr., of the University of South Carolina for reading and making suggestions about the manuscript. All responsibility for the completed work is of course my own.

The University of Alabama   CHARLES S. WATSON

FOREWORD

It would appear, after only a cursory thought or two, to be a relatively simple matter to write about American dramatists and their contributions to literature and theatre in America. But for almost the first one hundred and fifty years of the new republic the American dramatist was the object of such varied emotional outbursts by both audiences and critics or would-be critics that his status and even his existence is sometimes difficult to determine. He was ignored, derided, tolerated, exploited, or treated with such contempt that for many decades his position was scarcely to be envied. From the early days the English and Loyalists scorned his efforts; snobbish audiences might drive his play from the stage if the author acknowledged his American nationality; the theatre managers, who were mainly transplanted Englishmen, generally kept his plays from the public; and the literary elitists denied his creations the common label of literature. Religious detractors were only the best known from among the institutions or social forces in America that made the work of the American dramatist and that of his colleagues in the theatre difficult to bear. Consequently, many American dramatists have been denied their just places in the history of theatre and dramatic literature in America while their contributions have long since disappeared from readily available printed material if, indeed, their plays were printed at all. Writing about American drama is rarely an easy task.

No work, however, is completely victimized by negation and an overwhelming gloom. The American drama had its enthusiastic supporters soon after the nineteenth century got under way. Henry Adams noted that with the appearance in 1815 of the *North Amer-*

ican Review the prevailing attitude toward a literature that could be called American gradually experienced a change. With the more substantial plea in Ralph Waldo Emerson's *The American Scholar,* 1837, a recognition of American arts and letters began, and the drama reaped some, if slight, advantage through the increasingly meaningful contributions in poetry, fiction, and the essay. For the next fifty years American efforts in these genres far outstripped the work in drama, and this uneven advance bothered some of the late nineteenth century writers such as William Dean Howells, Mark Twain, and Henry James. All tried to write plays, and with the exception of Howells all failed in the theatre. But by this time both theatre and literary people were trying to make American society aware of an American drama. Essays in popular journals by men like Augustin Daly, Dion Boucicault, James A. Herne, Howells, and Brander Matthews appeared under such titles as "The American Dramatist," "American Playwrights on the American Drama," "The Future of American Drama," "The Characteristics of American Drama," or "The Relationship of Drama to Literature." It was slow in coming, but a consciousness of the drama was appearing in literary America—although few of the literati would accept it as a reality until after 1916.

A comprehensive and scholarly history of American drama has not yet been written, and there are a number of reasons why this rather deplorable void exists in the story of American letters. Foremost among these reasons would be the decided lack of interest in the academic world among those who might be expected to undertake the task and the general slowness in that same world to recognize value in its native literature. Emerson was not alone in asking for an awareness of American literature while his most distinguished adversaries were secreted behind ivy-covered walls promoting the classical tradition in which they themselves had been nurtured. By 1855 Duyckinck still insisted in his *Cyclopedia of American Literature* that literary work in America was only an adjunct of English literature. Not until after World War I did academia seriously consider teaching a literature that might be called American solely on its own merit, and it took a second World War before an abundance of Ph.D. candidates decided to concentrate upon American literature. Yet this literature was poetry, novel, short story, and essay. Among literary genres American drama has been the last to be generally accepted as a legitimate emphasis in the academic world, and the major reason given has been the poor quality of the dramas generally written by Americans during the eighteenth and nineteenth centuries—which explains the lack of interest among scholars.

It is difficult to argue with the conclusion that most of the early plays had slight literary quality. Yet a few antebellum dramas warrant literary analysis, and in the years prior to 1828 and the Prize Plays in America, a number of the plays written carry a literary quality comparable to that expressed by the poets and fiction writers of the time. It seems logical, too, that any art form has a history and that a literary historian assumes the burden of discovering and assessing the antecedents of modern American drama. There is, of course, no lack of comment on modern drama and this again is clearly understandable. The drama is always "now" in the theatre, just as life is always "now" for most people, and the "now" is always interesting. Added to this continuing attitude was the rise of the "New Criticism" after World War I and the lessening effect of literary historians in academic circles. Then, after Eugene O'Neill gained a reputation as a playwright, scholars around the world became interested in what was going on in American drama. When an English critic named Lawrence Kitchen declared after World War II that America was now a "potent intruder" in world drama, both critics and scholars in America found some satisfaction in the works of Arthur Miller and Tennessee Williams as well as a beginning for American drama in the plays of O'Neill—an observation which they accept from another English critic named William Archer. With a modern basis established for writing about American drama, it became increasingly difficult for anyone to venture back into the eighteenth or nineteenth centuries. Arguments that Amercian drama might have begun with Hunter's *Androboros* in 1714, Tyler's *Contrast* in 1787, or even Herne's *Margaret Fleming* more than a century later in 1890 have been extremely difficult to intrude upon biases that have been working against the acceptance of an American drama since the period of the Revolution—instituted and maintained by the same elitism which irritated Emerson in 1837.

The scholars and researchers who have shown some interest in American drama have been the theatre historians. Their concern for dates and factual information with reference to theatre buildings, managers, actors and actresses, and innumerable play productions has provided a valuable background for the historian of American drama. They have also supplied a great deal of evidence to explain and substantiate the prevailing biases by actors, managers, and critics, and audiences against the work of the American dramatist. But the historian of American theatre is not the historian of American drama. He does not have the same obligations and objectives nor is his task as limited as that of the historian of American drama. Contemporary criticism also favored the writer of theatre history. Reviewers discussed the production of the play, the manners or effectiveness of the actors, and the condition of the theatre. They provided comments on the plot of the play and perhaps gave the entire plot. Very rarely before the late nineteenth century did the reviewer assume the responsibilities of the drama critic and pass knowledgeable judgment on the play being performed. By far the majority of the published research on plays written by Americans before 1816 has been concerned with the particulars of production. Even those who have seemingly specialized in the history of American drama (Arthur Hobson Quinn, Montrose Moses, Margaret Mayorga) have felt it necessary to include a great deal of theatre history in their books—an emphasis upon actors, acting companies, managers and their theatres.

Although the value of research into the theatre as part of America's past is undeniable, a combination of attitudes and situations has confused the general appreciation of the drama and its creators who are equally a part of America's past. Clearly, the lives and performances of the actors and the problems of staging plays during the eighteenth and nineteenth centuries in America have proved far more interesting to a reading public than some of the dull literary plays or the abundance of slight hack work produced for an evening's entertainment. It is also clear that the majority of the plays printed warrant rather little serious literary analysis—to overstate a point. But to assume that American drama during these centuries has value only as social or historical documents is to allow worn out prejudices to rule good judgment. To accept the empty idea that there is no American drama worthy of the name prior to the work of O'Neill is another exercise of thoughtless bias. Exciting nights in the theatre would have been far less numerous during those decades if no Americans had been moved to write plays.

Although the lack of a first-rate American dramatist in the nineteenth century provides ample evidence for those who may condemn the entire drama of the period, it was, given the conditions in America, literally impossible for such a writer to appear. (In fact, that first-rate dramatist did not appear before Shaw during the same period in England.) English theatre managers and copyright problems discouraged some American dramatists. The demeaning position as a hack writer and the control exercised by the star system discouraged others. When Bronson Howard finally became the first dramatist to be able to make his career as a playwright, his expressed antipathy to all writers of some literary reputation who showed an interest in writing for the theatre only widened the existing gap between writers for the theatre and those who wrote fiction or poetry. William Gillette's declaration that no one could "read a play"; one could only read the "directions" for a play also worked to the disadvantage of those like William Dean Howells and Brander Matthews who wanted to find some relationship between drama and literature. But by this time, how-

ever, the twentieth century had begun; a dramatist named Clyde
Fitch had become a millionaire; America was becoming more involved in the affairs of a world where dramatists and theatre people worked together with excellent results; and the Little Theatre
movement in America was creating a need for playwrights who
would be recognized on their own merits. Nearly a hundred years
previously an actor named Edwin Forrest had asked Americans
to write plays for him, but intervening changes in both acting and
theatre techniques now brought the dramatist a recognition which
Edwin Forrest and others had denied him.

The full story of American drama, filled with inherent problems
and long delayed by intolerable but easily explained prejudices,
deserves its place with the histories of other literary genres in
America. Some fine beginnings have been made for that history
of American drama, but these are now a quarter of a century old,
and new material has become available during that time. Generally, the history of American drama is being written in bits and
pieces appearing in Ph.D. dissertations and journal essays. Most
of these contributions to a history are simply a part of the innumerable particulars which must be assessed before the synthesis can
be attempted. Occasionally, there is the study of an area or period
of time that offers substantive scope for drama analysis. Such a
study is the present one—the *Antebellum Charleston Dramatists*
by Charles S. Watson.

For the first quarter of the nineteenth century no city in America seemed to hold greater promise for the drama of America than
Charleston. With a perceptive drama critic in Stephen Cullen
Carpenter, a management which was not afraid to produce American plays, and a dozen dramatists whose works were produced on
its stage, Charleston was a major area of theatrical activity with
an especial tolerance for American plays. But after the 1820's
Charleston ceased to grow as a city, while more northern cities
like New York and Philadelphia took over the lead in theatrical
production, and the great potential was never achieved. Prof. Wat-

son presents this important period in an attractive manner and with the authority that excellent research makes possible. It is his thesis that the Charleston dramatists of the antebellum years helped form the American drama that was slowly asserting itself. No one should argue with his approach. Although Charleston produced no great dramatists, it most certainly provided the activity and the audience interest from which an American drama would eventually develop. Prof. Watson's work is one of the studies which must be appreciated if the unfolding history of American drama is to be meaningful and complete.

Department of   WALTER J. MESERVE
Theatre and Drama
Indiana University
Bloomington

PREFACE

As the United States devises plans to observe fittingly the bi-centennial year, 1976, it is clear that much still needs to be done in understanding the early development of our nation. In the field of early American drama much remains to be done. One subject long recognized as significant is the theatre of Charleston, South Carolina. It has drawn the attention of numerous scholars.[1] Books, articles, and dissertations have dealt with this subject sufficiently to show the vital position held by the Charleston theatre in the South and the United States from the colonial period to the Civil War. The dramatic writing for its stage, nevertheless, has not received commensurate attention. Strong appeals have been made to rectify this omission.[2]

My purpose is, first, to fill a clearly recognized need in regard to dramatic writing for the Charleston theatre and, second, to further the general understanding of early American drama. The group of plays composed for the Charleston theatre forms the largest and most cohesive body of dramatic writing for any theatre in the South before the Civil War. Like much early American drama, however, its meaning for contemporary audiences, and hence its true significance, has been lost. My principal conclusion in regard to methodology for early American drama is that it is imperative to know the historical events of the particular time in which a play was composed in order to comprehend its meaning for a contemporary audience. Sometimes a precise knowledge of local history and of the relations of theatre manager and dramatist is indispensable. With all this information at hand, the full significance of the play reveals itself, but not before. My approach in this study is based on that conviction. This approach has not been taken heretofore for one theatre over an extended period of time.

It has been known that there was considerable dramatic writing for the Charleston theatre before the Civil War. It has not been known what the nature of this dramatic writing was in fact. An understanding of the drama written for this stage brings to light the political and social views which found expression in this most representative and important theatre in the antebellum South. The plays present a panorama of change from nationalistic Jeffersonian Republicanism to support of Southern goals in the sectional struggle before the Civil War. They demonstrate cogently that the theatre served as a political platform reflecting the predominant view of its audience. Three names emerge from the dramatists for the Charleston stage as most significant. William Ioor, John Blake White, and William Gilmore Simms (known for his fiction but not sufficiently for his drama) composed plays that form an integral part of the long course of Southern literature. In their works appear some of the first manifestations of such features as agrarianism, typical Southern characters, and preoccupation with regional history, politics, and problems that have continued to characterize Southern literature. By their efforts, these dramatists contributed an essential part to the inauguration of American drama.

I

THE CHARLESTON
THEATER

rom its beginning early in
the eighteenth century till
1825 the theatre in Charleston, South Carolina, was active and important. The city initiated an enduring interest in the theatre with its first production of a play in 1735. For the remainder of the century Charleston had popular theatrical seasons and was the Southern linchpin of the traveling companies. From 1800 to 1825, the city ranked as one of the four theatrical centers of the United States, the others being New York, Philadelphia, and Boston.[1] After 1825, the Charleston theatre had violent swings from depression to prosperity, and dramatic writing declined in contrast to its flourishing from 1793 to 1825. The city, nevertheless, maintained a vital interest in the theatre. A survey of the theatre from the pre-Revolutionary era to the Civil War, including its managers and its relations with politics, newspapers, and local dramatists will provide the context for understanding writing for the Charleston theatre during this time. The politicization of the theatre will be particularly noted since that is the most significant historical fact to emerge from this study.

1

1703–1825

In the pre-Revolutionary period the city was served by traveling companies of English actors, like Lewis Hallam's and David Douglass's. In this period there are only a few indications of original writing for the theatre in Charleston and no plays have survived. Such writing would have to await a resident stock company and more leisure time among the city's inhabitants. A few records show the paucity of attempts to write for the stage. Anthony Aston, a soldier, came to Charleston in January, 1703. He fell back on his talents as a strolling player, wrote a play "on the Subject of the Country," and presented it to the people of the city. The contents of his play are unknown.[2] The David Douglass Company presented *Young America in London*, April 22, 1774, in Charleston. George O. Seilhamer believed this was by a Charlestonian.[3]

The first dramatic season began on January 18, 1735, with Thomas Otway's *The Orphan* in the city courtroom. The next year a theatre opened in Dock Street with Farquhar's *The Recruiting Officer*, and drama had truly made its start in Charleston.[4] The city was visited by the leading touring companies thereafter in the eighteenth century. Lewis Hallam's company came in 1754. David Douglass's troup arrived next for three seasons; its 1773–74 season was "the most brilliant" of colonial days in Charleston, according to Eola Willis.[5]

The theatre in Charleston is most interesting and significant from 1793 to 1825. At this time the theatre was a very popular place of entertainment, there was an able stock company, and there was a considerable amount of original writing for the local stage by residents of the community. Furthermore, the theatre was a vigorous political and patriotic platform during this period of Federalist-Republican controversy. Here as elsewhere, it expressed political ideas of the community that made it a significant barometer of public opinion.

The political situation in the nation from 1790 to 1825 is the

THE PRESENT DOCK STREET THEATRE,
A RESTORATION OF THE NINETEENTH CENTURY PLANTER'S HOTEL.
RESIDENT THEATRE FOR THE FOOTLIGHT PLAYERS.
COURTESY, EMMETT ROBINSON.

most important background for understanding the milieu of the Charleston theatre and its dramatists of this time. Above all there was the fierce conflict between Federalists and Republicans till 1816 when the last Federalist presidential candidate was nominated. South Carolina became increasingly Republican and pro-Jefferson in sentiment, and this view is the dominant one in the theatre of Charleston. There existed a strong Federalist element, however, especially in Charleston and many leaders of the state were Federalists, like Charles Cotesworth Pickney and John Rutledge. The Federalists were strongest in South Carolina in 1798 during a short time of anti-French feeling, but after 1800 with the election of Jefferson there was no question that the state was strongly Republican. It should be noted that the theatre of Charleston nevertheless would have to meet the opposition of powerful political and social leaders when it offered Republican productions.

The central political fact concerning the Charleston theatre from 1790 to the War of 1812 was the debate over our relations with Great Britain. Essentially the main thrust of the political plays written for the theatre favored what the Democratic-Republicans advocated when they called the War of 1812 the "Second War of Independence." That is, they wanted full independence from Britain and respectful treatment in international affairs. For example, Great Britain should recognize the right of its subjects to choose American citizenship without fear of impressment back into British sovereignty. The realization of this period as one in which the United States was attempting to confirm its complete independence of Britain clarifies much of the dramatic writing for the Charleston theatre since the dramatists joined the effort to achieve recognition of America as a fully independent nation by its former overlord.

Theatre in Charleston from 1793 to 1825 is best followed through its three most important managers: Thomas Wade West, Alexander Placide, and Charles Gilfert. The first impresario, West, an Englishman, established headquarters at Norfolk.[6] He initiated a Southern Circuit that continued to 1825 and included Richmond, Charleston, Savannah, and lesser towns. He deserves much credit for strengthening the theatre in the South.[7] In 1793 West opened a new theatre in Charleston, which lasted until 1833. It was spoken of nostalgically as the Old Charleston Theatre in later times.

This theatre, which was the stage for plays written by Charlestonians during the last decade of the eighteenth century and the first three decades of the nineteenth century, had been well planned by West to serve the city's future needs. The theatre which West and James Hoban built in 1793 was a plain, unadorned brick structure on the outside and remained so until 1830. The inside however was elaborate. Robert Mills, the architect of the George Washington Monument, and a former student of James Hoban, described the Charleston Theatre as it looked around 1826: "The theatre is a large building, without any architectural display outwardly, which is a rather remarkable circumstance here, as the citizens of Charleston have always been patrons of the muse of poetry and song. . . .The interior of this building presents a great contrast to the present exterior. It is arranged with taste, and richly decorated; the tout ensemble produces a handsome effect."[8] In 1830, a scene designer-architect, J. Sera, reworked the front, adding a portico with columns, which gave the theatre an impressive and attractive appearance. In 1833 the Charleston Theatre was sold to the Medical College of South Carolina.[9]

In the heated political atmosphere that existed from 1793, when the Charleston Theatre opened, until 1796, when West left, there is considerable evidence that West was decidedly cool to the pro-French, Republican tendency that was raging in Charleston. In December, 1793, there appeared a request in the newspaper to Mr. West. The writer stated that his friend, a citizen, was the author of "The Americans and French at the Siege of Yorktown, or The Surrender to Cornwallis," a national piece. The writer offered it "to your stage for exhibition."[10] West did not produce this composi-

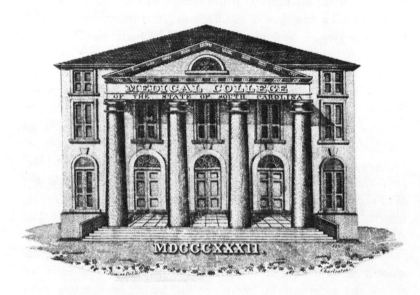

OLD CHARLESTON THEATRE, BUILT IN 1793, AFTER IT
WAS CONVERTED TO A MEDICAL COLLEGE.
COURTESY, EMMETT ROBINSON.

tion.[11] Shortly after West opened the Charleston Theatre in 1793 his theatre was named specifically in a letter to the *National Gazette* as an example of the pro-aristocratic American theatre, which exhibited the theatrical foppery of passionate Kings, pouting Queens, rakish Princes, and flirting Princesses."[12] George C. Rogers,, Jr., notes that plays considered arisocratic like *The Life and Death of Mary Queen of Scots* were produced at West's theatre and states that it was this theatre which the Federalists attended.[13] West's non-production of pieces about the American Revolution, the contrasting zest for them at the newly opened French Theatre, his offerings of plays about royalty and his English background point to the conclusion that he sympathized with the Federalist, pro-British faction in Charleston. The theatre under his management thus reflected the Federalist strength in Charleston at this time.

In the early 1790's, Charleston received a substantial number of French immigrants who were destined to have a vitalizing influence on the city's life and especially on the theatre. One of their number, Alexander Placide, a celebrated dancer and tight rope acrobat, would emerge as the impresario of Charleston's theatrical activities at the end of the decade. In 1791 there was a slave rebellion on Santo Domingo and many Frenchmen fled and came to Charleston.[14] Their arrival brought talented people in theatrical entertainment to the city and provided an audience for a French theatre. Three years later conditions were ripe for the opening of a French theatre. On April 10, 1794, the day the French Theatre opened, Messrs. Placide and Val applied to William Hort, Treasurer of the City Council, for a license to exhibit "theatrical entertainments" for the following year. They received a license on payment of 100 pounds sterling. A letter in the newspaper referred to Placide as in charge of performances at the French Theatre, hence the manager. The opening night of the French Theatre, April 10, 1794, included *Pygmalion*, *The Three Philosophers*, and dancing on the tight rope by Signor Spinacuta and Placide. The announcement in the newspaper began with the statement that "the Theatre will be opened for the benefit of the American Prisoners in Algiers."[15] The French management knew it was wise to open with a cause popular in a city desiring commerce free of interference from the Barbary pirates. The French Theatre became known as the City Theatre (sometimes called also the Church Street Theatre). Its opening marked the beginning of competition with the Charleston Theatre.

A principal fact about the French actors in Charleston is their revolutionary spirit and sponsorship of pieces praising the American and French Revolutions. By their productions of original pageants celebrating Britain's defeat and the victory of republican ideas, they demonstrated forcefully the use of the theatre as a political platform.

The revolutionary spirit was evident at the opening of the French Theatre, April 10, 1794. Charles Fraser described this event and said his "liveliest recollection" of the theater was the "frantic enthusiasm" of the privateermen's singing when the orchestra played the "Marseillois" and "Ça ira."[16] A number of original productions glorifying the American and French Revolutions were presented. Such spectacles in the 1790's were *ipso facto* anti-British. On June 28, 1794, Placide, already known as a composer of pantomimes and manager of the French Theatre, planned a patriotic spectacle, *Attack on Fort Moultrie.* The anniversary of this battle was a patriotic holiday for South Carolinians and especially for Charlestonians, where church bells are still rung on June 28. In this battle Sgt. William Jasper raised the flag at peril of his life saying, "Let us not fight without a flag." This spectacle was performed on July 1, 2, 4, and August 4, 1974, and was also called "The 28th of June 1776." A newspaper stated there would be "a grand Military and Patriotic Pantomine in two acts, never performed here, called The 28th of June, 1776, or ATTACK ON FORT MOULTRIE." It would be presented at the French Theatre in Church Street and the end would be an allegorical feast in honor of the "Brave American Heroes."

Liberty was to be played by Madame Douvillier and America by Madame Val.[17]

Trying to duplicate the success of *Attack on Fort Moultire,* Placide and the noted scene painter Audin presented a new pantomime, *American Independence or the 4th of July 1776,* presented on July 30, 1794, at the French Theatre. The spectable was described as a patriotic pantomime with an allegorical prologue.[18]

Even when the French actors went over to the Charleston Theatre they continued these patriotic spectacles. Because West's theatre suffered from the popularity of the French actors, he arranged for them to perform at the Charleston Theatre in the fall of 1794 at the beginning of the 1794-95 season. One of the conditions of the French actors arrangement with the Charleston Theatre was that on every Saturday night they would present a French program. Consequently on November 14, 1794, a Saturday, Mr. Francisqui and Placide presented a historical pantomime on the fall of the Bastille entitled *The 14th of July, 1789.* The pantomime showed the demolition of the prison and the freeing of "the unfortunate prisoners."[19]

In February, 1795, a former member of West's troupe, Hayden Edgar, planned an anti-monarchical play, *Louis XVI,* at the French Theatre, where he had gone to be manager. His choice was attacked in the press. "T.R.," a correspondent of the *Tea-Table or Evening Gazette,* had found some speeches in the drama offensive to the true republican spirit. Mr. Edgar answered that he suspected the correspondent was "of the other theatre or employed by it." He said he had removed offensive speeches in rehearsal. He admitted, however, that in a tragedy there are two parties and the death of Louis XVI "shews which party it was meant to please." He does not think that "true republicanism" consists of violence but believes that "calm" measures will settle a republican government on a firm basis; such measures are "plainly exemplyfied [sic] in the present national assembly of France." He has consulted with "some men of true republican principles" and they wish to see it performed. *Louis XVI* was presented at the City Theatre, February 11,

12, and 14, 1795.[20] This statement by Edgar is important because it indicates definite political differences between the theatres.

In 1795 the patriotic pageant about the siege of Yorktown that had been rejected by West in 1793 was presented by the French actors. On April 30, 1795, "The Siege of Yorktown" by the Rev. John Paul Coste, pastor of the Huguenot church, was given at the Charleston Theatre after West had vacated the theatre at the end of the season. The author had repeatedly asked West and his partner, John Bignall, an English actor, to produce it. The scenery showed "the British men of war firing on the besieged." The pageant was dedicated to the Battalion of Charleston.[21]

These patriotic spectacles composed specifically for the local theatres mark the real beginning of original writing for the theatre in Charleston. It should be noted that these original productions were called forth in a time of strong political feeling and handed to a friendly and receptive company. The theatre was clearly seen as a platform to arouse political sentiment in the city. The predominant tone in the original pieces of this time is pro-revolutionary and hence pro-Republican rather than pro-Federalist.

Consistent with its staging of patriotic spectacles, the French-directed company in Charleston contributed to an important development in American drama at this time: the popularization of the battle play. In July, 1797, the new manager of the company, John Sollee, a Frenchman, announced that he had concluded an agreement whereby there would be an exchange of actors with the Haymarket Theatre of Boston. Boston actors would appear in Charleston, and Charleston actors in Boston. On February 20, 1797, the Boston company had performed *The Battle of Bunker Hill* by John Daly Burk, the first full-fledged battle play to become a success in America. The scene painter for the Charleston company, Audin, had done the scenery. Burk had next asked John Hodgkinson in New York to present his play, but was turned down. Hodgkinson had been told by John B. Williamson, manager of the Federal St. Theatre in Boston (the Federalist theatre) that the play was "execrable," although from its *"peppering"* the British had brought full houses to the Haymarket (the Republican theatre). Sollee's new company of Boston and Charleston actors, however, presented *Bunker Hill* at the John St. Theatre of New York in September, 1797. William Dunlap ridiculed the play and the performance in that city. On returning to Charleston, Sollee's company performed *Bunker Hill* on January 8, 1798 at the Charleston Theatre. The actors were mainly from Charleston with a few from Boston. The play was again presented at the City Theatre on February 14, 1799. After Alexander Placide became the sole manager of the Charleston Theatre, he made *Bunker Hill* a standby in the company's repertoire. It was performed in 1801, 1802, 1804, and 1808.[22]

After its successful launching by the combined efforts of the Boston and Charleston companies, *Bunker Hill* became a highly popular play on the American stage for many years. Coinciding with its popularity, the battle play became one of the most numerous and popular types of plays by American dramatists. *Bunker Hill* and later battle plays had a broad appeal and played a vital part in the democratization of the American drama. The form was extremely versatile since it could serve to celebrate a holiday, keep alive a historic event, and arouse popular sentiment on a controversial issue. The Charleston company, under its French management, helped substantially in the promotion of the battle play and thus exhibited the egalitarian philosophy and Republican political view that was changing American life in this Jeffersonian era. Continuing the city's affinity for this type of play, Charleston's three leading dramatists, William Ioor, John Blake White, and William Gilmore Simms, composed battle plays.

The most important figure to emerge from the turbulent years of theatre rivalry and political conflict in the 1790's was Alexander Placide (1750–1812), who became sole manager of the Charleston Theatre on March 31, 1800, and held that position during the most flourishing period of the theatre in Charleston. Placide was born Alexandre-Placide Bussart in Paris, though he never used his last name in America. He had enjoyed considerable success in France and Great Britain before coming to the United States. Though he was known best as a rope dancer and acrobat with the famous troupe of Nicolet, by 1772 he was composing and staging pantomimes. In Europe he composed and staged at least eleven pantomimes, and in America more than twenty-five. In England during the American Revolution he waved the French flag before an audience and received a cudgeling. This incident is consistent with his later production of American and French Revolutionary spectacles in Charleston. Placide arrived in Santo Domingo in 1788 where he and Madame Placide performed four years before coming to the United States. His first recorded performance in this country was in New York, June 5, 1792.[23]

Under Placide's management, Charleston became the headquarters for the Southern Circuit since the company serving the area made its residence there. Placide is particularly interesting because during his management the largest number of plays by Charlestonians were produced: seven in all, among which were two by William Ioor, three by John Blake White, and one by Isaac Harby. To know something of the personality of a showman like Placide is to recapture some of the theatrical life in this early period of the Old South. He appeared in Charleston as "the first Rope Dancer to the King of France."[24] William Dunlap called the team of Mr. and Mrs. Placide "powerful," the husband in dance and pantomine, the wife in acting and singing.[25] The beauty of Mrs. Placide was much admired, and on one occasion her husband killed the lover of his wife in a duel. It was fought with "short swords behind the Tobacco Inspection in Charleston."[26]

Placide used his varied talents to the full in Charleston. In his reminiscences of the Charleston theatre, Dr. John Beaufain Irving recalls that Placide was very fond of pantomines and often acted in them.[27] Eola Willis says that Placide and the noted scene painter Audin, both of whom loved pageantry, often collaborated on the spectacular staging of pantomine. She adds that Placide arranged all the dances and undoubtedly was the highest paid member of the cast when he performed with West's company.[28]

One of Placide's most popular performers was Matthew Sully, his partner in pantomimes. Sully acted the harlequin to Placide's clown and used to delight "the children that were young, and children that were old" by jumping through a clock and doing other marvelous things.[29] Another example of Sully's gymnastics came at the conclusion of the performance of William Ioor's *Battle of Eutaw Springs*. According to a newspaper notice, after the epilogue to this drama, Mr. Sully would "leap through the WORLD, surrounded by BRILLIANT FIREWORKS."[30]

During his years as sole manager of the Charleston Theatre, Placide continued to show his liking for revolutionary and hence pro-Republican dramas; these plays were loudly patriotic. Placide produced John Daly Burk's *The Battle of Bunker Hill,* the vociferous Republican drama, many times. John B. Williamson, a co-manager in Charleston with Placide, had condemned this play in 1797 for appealing to "the prevailing Jacobin spirit in the lower ranks."[31] Placide also produced the pro-Republican plays of the local dramatist William Ioor: *Independence* (1805 and 1806) and *The Battle of Eutaw Springs* (1807 and 1808). His purpose of making the theatre a patriotic platform appeared further in such offerings as *Liberty in Louisiana* (1804), celebrating the Louisiana Purchase; *Bombardment of Tripoli* (1805) and *Burning of the Frigate Philadelphia in the Harbor of Tripoli* (1806), in honor of the Americans fighting against the Barbary pirates; and *Birthday of the Immortal Washington* (February 22, 1812).[32]

The harshest criticism of Placide was made by Isaac Harby, journalist, playwright, and dramatic critic. In his newspaper, *The Quiver,* he lauded a play by William Maxwell of Savannah, "which Mr. Placide, the theatrical carver for the public taste in Charleston has *put off,* for the stuff of Dibdin, Cherry and O'Keefe—We are to be amused with harlequinades, Elephants, and Cinderellas, while the soft and sentimental efforts of Maxwell are hindered from their proper sphere of exhibition!"[33]

We may conclude from these comments by Harby that Placide presented a great deal of frivolous, spectacular entertainment. Nevertheless, he seems to have tried to increase the number of plays by the best English dramatists. Certainly, over a period of several years, a Charlestonian would have been able to see a variety of Shakespeare, the standard repertory pieces like Otway's *Venice Preserved,* and works by influential contemporary writers like Kotzebue and M. G. Lewis. The last two would have exposed him to such movements as sentimentalism and Gothicism.

Placide died in 1812 in New York City, the year after his company suffered a disastrous fire at the Richmond Theatre on December 23, 1811.[34] He was subsequently described as a person of "most extraordinary accomplishments" whether considered as "a dancer on the tight rope, in which he had no rival, as a manager, or as a man of wonderful mind and resources."[35]

The last important manager of this period was Charles Gilfert (1787–1829). He was the son-in-law of Joseph G. Holman, a man of "education, accomplishments, and taste," who directed the theatre for two seasons, 1815–16 and 1816–17.[36] Gilfert managed the theatre from 1817 to 1825 and resembled Placide in being a flamboyant figure who brought a vitality to the town's theatrical life that would be fondly remembered. Though Gilfert had periods of financial difficulty, he was working during a time when the Southern Circuit maintained a lively existence and before regional theatrical activity was reduced by centralization of the theatre in New York.

A contrast of the theater under Placide and Gilfert should be noted. The theatre continued to be a patriotic platform but declined as a political platform since controversial plays by local residents virtually disappeared. Patriotic observances included performances of *The Battle of New Orleans,* January 8, 1818, and *The Battle of Bunker Hill,* May 9, 1821. Local dramatists, however, wrote plays that were non-controversial. Isaac Harby's *Alberti,* presented for President James Monroe in 1819, was patriotic in praising American independence and democratic government, but not politically controversial.

Gilfert came from Germany to Charleston as a young man. He opened a "musical establishment," played in the Philharmonic Society Orchestra, directed the theatre orchestra, and otherwise identified himself with the musical life of the city.[37] Biographical material contains criticism of his personal life but praise for his work as a theatre manager. Dr. Irving terms Gilfert's marriage to Agnes Holman, daughter of the manager, "ill-judged." Calling the young lady "well-educated and refined," he says that Gilfert was a man "of all others least suited to her education, habits, and associations." This manager had a reputation for gambling and would "go his pile upon a card."[38] According to one source, he was "regardless of obligation and reckless in money matters."[39] Before his marriage, Gilfert had once shown too much attention to the wife of Charley Young, a popular actor of the stock company; afterward the two men engaged in a duel at the Charleston Race Grounds, in which Young was wounded in the hip.[40]

Other details on Gilfert present a more complimentary picture. In the early days of his management, he lived in a house dubbed "Brandenburg Castle," where he entertained the patrons of the theatre in Charleston. The "choice spirits of the Day" met there, including Isaac Harby, "a fine Belle Lettre scholar," who was the author of two produced plays and a newspaper reviewer of the drama. Dr. Irving says that Gilfert later resided in a good suite of apartments in "the old Theatre." His distinctive personality was caricatured in a performance of *Tom and Jerry* on March 1, 1824, when an actor imitated Gilfert by peering over his spectacles in a manner that convulsed the audience with laughter.[41]

When Gilfert took over from Holman in 1817, he had difficulty reviving interest in the stage. One means tried during the first season was the presentation of a local writer's work, Edwin Holland's version of Byron's *Corsair,* with special music by Gilfert. Toward the end of this season Thomas A. Cooper an English-born actor popular in Charleston, had a great success. In 1818–19, the season started badly, and Gilfert followed Placide's example of visiting Savannah for a few weeks. In April of this season the theatre was the scene of a memorable event, the attendance of President James Monroe while on an official visit to Charleston. On the president's second night at the theatre, *Alberti,* a play by Isaac Harby, was proudly offered.[42] Gilfert's company made tours in Virginia from 1819 to 1823. It has been called "the most important company on the Richmond stage between 1819 and 1838."[43]

Two events that occurred during Gilfert's last season should be mentioned. In March, 1825, Lafayette visited Charleston and attended the theatre as part of his tour of the nation. Gilfert offered for that occasion Samuel Woodworth's *Lafayette, or the Castle of Olmutz,* a drama about a South Carolinian's attempt to rescue the French hero from a German prison.[44] There was a military ball at the theatre in Lafayette's honor on March 16, 1825. Shortly afterwards, the company gave the first performance of *Fauntleroy,* written by one of its members, John Augustus Stone.[45] Stone later was the author of *Metamora,* the Indian play made famous by Edwin Forrest.

The tributes paid Gilfert for his work in Charleston show that whatever his personal failings, he left behind many accomplishments. Dr. Irving remarks that a new era started with Gilfert; he engaged a strong company and held it together. Stars could rely on being well supported by his company.[46] Speaking of the whole antebellum period, W. Stanley Hoole concludes that perhaps no man advanced theatrical art in the city as Gilfert did.[47]

The facts, figures, and personalities for the Charleston stage from 1800 to 1825 mark these years as significant and memorable. Dr. Irving speaks of this era as "the palmy days of the old Broad-street Theatre." He states that at this time "the Theatre was generally prosperous and the companies good."[48]

Besides vigorous theatrical management during the time of Placide and Gilfert, Charleston had frequent dramatic criticism in such newspapers as the *Courier*, the *City Gazette*, and the *Times*. The first important critic of this period was Stephen Cullen Carpenter, an Irishman, who was editor of the *Courier* and signed his reviews "Thespis."[49] Though considerable dramatic criticism had appeared in Charleston newspapers before 1800,[50] it is significant that Carpenter is named first in a list of local critics given by Dr. Irving.[51] Carpenter's reviews appeared in the *Courier* from March 30, 1803 to April 21, 1806. He also published the *Monthly Register, Magazine, and Review of the United States*, a national magazine, while in Charleston, and later the *Mirror of Taste and Dramatic Censor* in Philadelphia. For most of his residence this editor of the Federalist *Courier* seems to have remained non-partisan toward the drama. Only at the end of his stay are there signs that his political attitude came into question. This will be discussed below in the controversy which occurred in 1806 over the Republican play by William Ioor, *The Battle of Eutaw Springs*.

In his column for the *Courier*, Carpenter expressed his philosophy of the theatre and evaluated performances. Agreeing with the predominant view of his time, Carpenter's basic principle was that drama should be a school of morals. In his *Mirror of Taste and Dramatic Censor* he described drama as a "powerful moral agent" which may train us in our manners and deportment.[52] He had given expression to this view many times in the *Courier*. In his first essay, he stated that parents and the public should compel theatre managers to make the stage "a school of morals and manners for the rising generation." Since the drama so interests the heart, it must be "an instrument of astonishing force in moulding, training, and perfecting the dispositions of society" (March 30, 1803).

Another principle frequently mentioned by Carpenter is that characters should be true to nature. This idea had been stressed by eighteenth-century Scottish critics, who were influential in America.[53] In answer to a letter, "Thespis" wrote in the *Courier* on March 15,

1804, that for instruction to be effective dramatic personages must be drawn so that we may reasonably suppose they exist. They should speak and act, as Falstaff believed, like folks of this world.

Carpenter was particularly concerned with the performances and personal conduct of local actors. If they were negligent, he was quick to point out their errors. On May 24, 1804, "Thespis" scolded the actors for neglecting to study their lines and for their lack of sobriety. He said that neighbors of the theatre had complained to him about their conduct.

Carpenter made specific recommendations for improving the level of theatrical fare. On April 27, 1803, he wrote that actors can make up for the deficiencies of contemporary playwrights by drawing on the "inspired pieces of Shakespeare; on the luminous wit of Congreve" and on other earlier writers. After this criticism, made at the end of the 1802–03 season, signs of improvement appeared at the Charleston Theatre. In the following season, the number of evenings devoted to Shakespeare increased from three to seven. During 1805–06, the final season reviewed by Carpenter, Shakespearean plays were performed on fourteen evenings.[54]

It is evident from Carpenter's growing satisfaction with the company at the Charleston Theatre that its professional quality was improving and that he must have felt responsible in some measure. On the opening night of the second season which he reviewed, He praised a performance of M. G. Lewis's *Castle Spectre,* and remarked that the manager, Alexander Placide, had now gathered the best company yet to be seen on the Charleston boards (November 12, 1803). In "Thespis, No. III" for the last season of his reviewing, he devoted an entire essay to the company; he found the local troupe superior to any that he had seen in the best provincial theatres of England (November 20, 1805).

In the sixth essay for the 1805–06 season, "Thespis" praised his readers as well as the actors. There was less reason now to write criticism. His first purpose, to promote zeal for drama, had been accomplished. Since he had continually brought before readers the subject of drama, their judgment had emerged and they now engaged in discussions of plays on their own. Furthermore, the merit of the acting company now required little aid from the press (December 14, 1805).

Carpenter's support of local playwriting is especially noteworthy. In 1804 he reviewed favorably *Liberty in Louisiana* by James Workman, an Irishman then living in Charleston, who later became Judge of the County of Orleans, Louisiana. In the *Courer* for April 1, 1805, he praised the first play of South Carolina, William Ioor's *Independence*.

To honor *Independence,* Carpenter wrote a prologue.[55] It begins with a description of the first settlement of South Carolina and moves to a vision of future American literature. In the opening Carpenter refers clearly to the terrain around Charleston. Shakespeare, Congreve, and Otway were unknown

> When, midst entagled woods, and humid swamps,
> Expos'd to parching suns, and chilling damps,
> Your bold progenitors, with dangerous toil,
> Drew scanty bread, from out this sandy soil.

The race that settled here would not bow to "a tyrant shrine" but overcame that obstacle and others, such as "the Indian's Yew." Those troubles past, the mind found some time "for peaceful exercise." Carpenter then describes the spirit of America: "Columbia's Genius," with "hope prophetic" on her crest, watches "fair Science" advance. Columbia proclaims to Americans: "Art, Science, Poetry shall yet be thine; / Thine too the Drama." Carpenter then tells Americans of their future:

> At no distant age,
> Your own great deeds, shall yet adorn your Stage:
> And Shakespeares of your own hand down to fame,
> Each patriot's, sage's, statesman's honored name.
> Whether this prophecy has yet proved true

In any part, our author leaves to you.
He hopes this firstling of your native Stage,
Your fond paternal feelings will engage;
And, as in ardent fondness you have press'd
Your callow offspring, to your throbbing breast,
That you will take this to your tender care,
Its merits foster, and its errors spare.

The plea for support by "our author," that is, Ioor, was customary in this period.

In his last year in the city, Carpenter wrote an epilogue for the first tragedy of the state, John Blake White's *Foscari*. These verses were printed in the *Courier* on February 25, 1806. After Carpenter, dramatic criticsm continued to appear in the newspapers, sometimes in the form of letters from anonymous correspondents. Dr. Irving writes that from the first "there has always been some one well qualified to speak the praises of those upon the stage who merited particular commendation." He observes that

no *star* shone in darkness, and the darkness comprehended it not, as far as the public mind, *unsophisticated,* could be enlightened by judicious criticisms. Among others who might be cited in our community as having, from season to season, been distinguished for their dramatic writings, were Messrs. Carpenter, Momford, Edwin C. Holland, J. N. Cardozo, Isaac Harby, Wm. Crafts, and W. G. Simms.[56]

Near the end of his residence in Charleston, Carpenter was accused of obstructing native dramatic writing and being pro-aristocratic. Since the charge was from a Republican toward a well-known Federalist, it is clear that political enmity lay behind the statements. William Ioor wrote in the *City Gazette,* July 16, 1806 that Carpenter was opposing the publication of his play *The Battle of Eutaw Springs* .He accused Carpenter of this opposition because his "prediliction for every thing monarchical, every thing aristocratical has been notorious ever since he took his residence amongst us." Carpenter answered this letter in the *Courier*. He said that the insinuation of Ioor had been bandied about "a thousand times." He further stated that a play must have more to it than patriotism, that is, literary worth (July 19, 1806). The political motivation of this argument is confirmed by the newspaper reaction to the first performance of the play on January 10, 1807. The Republican *City Gazette* printed two communications on January 14, 1807, praising the piece, while the *Courier* completely ignored it. Though Carpenter was a genuine supporter of native dramatic writing and seems to have tried to remain non–partisan in his view of drama, some persons at least did not believe that he succeeded. His disagreement with Ioor is another clear sign of the political differences that existed at this time.

1826 to the Civil War

The theatre in Charleston from 1826 to 1860 remained a highly popular place of entertainment with long theatrical seasons, but it underwent a decline in terms of theatre management and production of plays by local dramatists. Contrasting the earlier with the later period William Gilmore Simms stated in 1869: "The drama continued to flourish in Charleston till about 1825."[57]

After Charles Gilfert left Charleston in 1825, the theatre had a succession of managers and financial truobles till 1833, when it was sold to the Medical College of South Carolina. For the 1827–28 season Dr. John B. Irving, active in literary and professional circles, was manager. Dr. Irving was obliged to close the season early because of pecuniary losses. Thomas Faulkner became manager in the 1830–31 season and brought Edwin Forrest to Charleston for his first performance.[58] This actor was a friend of Simms and the latter looked to him for assistance in dramatic writing. The last performance at the old Charleston Theatre was on April 1, 1833. The theatre was sold by the Proprietors in that year for $12,000, and it was reopened in November, 1834, as the Medical College of South Carolina. As the actor Tyrone Power wrote, the building originally designed for a theatre became a school of anatomy, "so *cutting up* is still the order of the day; only this practice is no longer confined to the poets, but extends to subjects generally."[59] When the old Charleston Theatre was sold, theatricals were transferred to the Queen Street Theatre, a barn-like structure, and Seyle's Long Room. Hoole calls these years, 1833–1836, the lowest point in Charleston theatricals from 1800 to the Civil War. Pantomimes, circuses, and musical productions predominated at this time, rather than legitimate drama.[60]

The next decade, 1837–1847, was much better as the city enjoyed prosperous times and the New Charleston Theatre opened in 1837. Exports of rice jumped from only 196,881 bushels in 1831 to 493,262 in 1839.[61] A group of local businessmen formed "The Charleston New Theatre Company," sold stock, and by April 20, 1837, announced its opening for next November. This building was in the popular Greek Revival style with a portico of Ionic columns and a seating capacity of 1200. According to Hoole there was nothing in the South that could surpass the New Charleston Theatre.[63]

The New Charleston Theatre open on December 15, 1837, to a crammed house. Dr. Irving wrote that W. H. Latham, the stage manager, came forward to "the most deafening applause." As soon as silence was restored, he delivered "a poetical address," by "my much admired friend, W. Gilmore Simms, Esq., the Poet Laureate of our State, as I have always called him."[64] William Abbott was the first manager and secured full houses. He started the opera seasons that were very popular until the Civil War. Hoole states that Abbott made Charleston an important theatrical center during his management.[65]

The next manager was William C. Forbes, 1842–1847, who is notable for the actors he engaged and his support of local play-writing. Dr. Irving praised Forbes as "an honest, courteous and indus-

THE "NEW" CHARLESTON THEATRE,
OPENED DECEMBER 15, 1837.

trious man." He stated that Forbes was "faithful and just in all his dealings, and was a very meritorious and painstaking actor, perfect to the letter."[66] Famous actors who gave Charleston excellent theatrical seasons at this time included J. B. Booth, William Charles Macready, Edwin Forrest, the native Charlestonian Henry Placide (son of the manager, Alexander Placide), James Hackett, and Anna Cora Mowatt, who performed in her own play *Fashion* four times in December, 1845.[67]

During the decline of Charleston dramatic writing, Forbes was the manager who promoted local talent most diligently. He presented the following pieces, which were either by Charlestonians or by anonymous writers who dealt with subjects of local interest and hence wrote specifically for this theatre: *De Montalt* (February 2, 1843) by James W. Simmons; *Siege of Charleston* (February 22, 23, 27, 1843); *The Spanish Exile* by A. J. Requier (March 28, April 1, 1844); *The Yemassee*, a dramatization of Simms's novel, (January 6, 7, 1845); and "Did you Ever Send Your Wife to Mount Pleasant?" (December 21, 1846 and January 19, 26, 1847).[68] Forbes, however, failed to produce a play submitted to him by Simms in 1844.[69]

The last phase before the Civil War, 1847–1861, comprised prosperous times for the city's economy but fluctuating periods for the theatre. New institutions were established, like the Museum of Natural History. Many journals were published in Charleston, such as Simms's *Southern Quarterly Review* and Paul Hamilton Hayne's *Russell's Magazine*. From October to December, 1851, F. C. Adams was manager; Simms wrote him without success about producing his play *Norman Maurice*. From 1852 to 1861, there were three managers: John Sloman (1852–53); John Sloan (1853–57); and G. F. Marchant (1857–61). For a number of years after 1853 the theatre was governed by "The Charleston Theatre Association" according to the *Courier* (April 17, 1854 and December 29, 1855).[70] Celebrated actors and singers appeared at the New Charleston Theatre during these years: Edwin Booth, Julia

Dean, the most popular actress in Charleston prior to the Civil War, and Jennie Lind. Opera and other musical entertainment offered competition at Harmony Hall. The New Charleston Theatre, which had begun in 1837, had its last performance on November 30, 1861, with drills by the Charleston Volunteers. [71]

Contemporary comments on the theatre reveal that this institution was at times the subject of lively controversy. In 1837, the Rev. Thomas Smyth opposed the opening of a new theatre in a pamphlet, *The Theater, A School of Religion, Manners, & Morals!* Smyth disapproved that a new theatre had been erected in the city at an expense of "about sixty thousand dollars." He questioned if this theatre could be "a school of morals" when such a character as "Harlequin ridicules heaven and exposes religion."[72]

The Rev. Smyth was answered by "Otway" in *The Theatre Defended. A Reply to Two Discourses of the Rev. Thomas Smyth.* He repeated Stephen Carpenter's point that the theatre was indeed a school of morals. This apologist wrote that since the opening of the "New Theatre" the taverns are almost wholly deserted by those who used to frequent them in the hours now devoted to "the play house." The theatre may not be as proper a place to obtain doctrines of religion as the church but it is a better school of morals than "the tavern." The villainies of Iago, the "holy innocence" of Desdemona, and "the end of the unhappy Moor" are an impressive lesson against jealousy.[73]

Another contemporary observer described the conflict of two social classes who attended the theatre at this time. The actor, Louis Fitzgerald Tasistro, wrote that there were two classes of theatre-goers in Charleston: first the "Mercantile" or business-professional class, which also included the better-paid mechanics; and, second, the "South Carolina Aristocracy," the large planters of the area. He wrote that the latter flock into Charleston around February and may be distinguished by their "fantastic, goatish beards" and "their propensity for aping European Continental manners," which render them "obnoxious" to the more "sedate and sensible portion of the community." Yet at the theatre everything is forgotten in the desire to please the latter class to the neglect of the former. This has resulted in the lack of support by the "Mercantile classes."[74] James H. Dormon notes that this policy by the Charleston Theatre might have reduced audiences. He remarks that in the United States at this time no manager could afford to neglect, much less offend, "*any* class" of the public he served.[75] Such an atmosphere may also have contributed to the decrease of political plays in Charleston from 1825 to 1860.

As reminiscents like Dr. John B. Irving and William Gilmore Simms wrote, the best days of the Charleston theatre were before 1825, mainly during the managements of Placide and Gilfert. Indeed, there were many financial and managerial troubles in the second period, but these had occurred before. What is also clear is that the theatre became more a place of imported acting talent and less a patron of original plays written by residents.

II

DRAMATIC WRITING,
1797 TO THE CIVIL WAR

Dramatic writing for the Charleston theatre may be divided into two periods. The first, from 1797 to 1825, including the managements of Placide and Gilfert was the most productive and reflected the vitality of the theatre. The second, from 1826 to the Civil War, was less fruitful, but continued the same tradition of local writing for the theatre. In the first period the most important dramatists were William Ioor and John Blake White; in the second, the principal dramatist was William Gilmore Simms, the only Charleston writer of the antebellum era to achieve national prominence. These men will be dealt with in separate chapters below. This chapter will describe in chronological order other dramatists of both periods. They illustrate the vitality and quantity of dramatic writing at this time.

1797–1825

Following the original spectacles and pantomimes presented in Charleston in the 1790's came the first plays to be published. The number of plays written for the Charleston theatre from the end of the eighteenth century to 1825 shows the vitality of dramatic writing at this time. With the addition of the most important dramatists, William Ioor and John Blake White, in the succeeding chapters, the nature of this activity will be realized. At the first of the period plays reflected the intense Federalist-Republican conflict. The predominance of the Republican view is attributable to the increasing strength of that party in South Carolina and the receptivity of Alexander Placide, manager of the Charleston Theatre. After the War of 1812 until the slavery controversy, plays tended to be non-partisan.

The political nature of the theatre during the Federalist-Republican struggle is found generally in the nation and is similar to the situation in Charleston. William Dunlap's *Andre* (1798) has a Federalist point of view and was presented in New York when pro-British feeling was strong. Pro-Republican dramas include *The Essex Junto,* published in Salem, Massachusetts, in 1802, and John Daly Burk's noisy crowd-pleaser, *The Battle of Bunker Hill,* first performed in Boston in 1797 and given repeatedly throughout the nation in subsequent years. Burk was a vigorous Republican who wrote other pro-Republican plays.

The first original piece given in Charleston that survived in print is an anti-British work. It is by John Beete, an actor. This comedy was performed at the City Theatre on April 24, 1797, as the author's benefit. An original play was often chosen for a benefit. It was published as "The Man of the Times: or A Scarcity of Cash. A Farce. As performed, with universal applause, at the Church-Street Theater, Charleston. Written by Mr. Beete, Comedian." Beete expressed his nationalistic feeling about dramatic writing in a statement "To the Public." He asked for support of persons who wish "to encourage native dramatic literature, so that our stage may not always exhibit foreign productions." This play presents England as a land of instruction in chincanery and dishonesty. Old Screwpenny has sent his son, Charles, there for an education in disreputable ways, but he has not adopted them. Screwpenny says in a soliloquy that his son has returned with contempt for everything except what he calls "honesty, sincerity, philanthropy, and such stuff."[1] Screwpenny asks his son where he learned such "nonsense," since he gave him letters to "noblemen." Charles replies that after seeing their "dissipation," he sickened with "their follies and vices."[2] According to the *Dramatis Personae*, Beete played the part of "Old Screwpenny."

The next work is a pro-French, Republican masque. It was presented February 9, 1798, at the Charleston Theatre when it was under the management of John Sollee. The work was published in 1802 as *Americana; or, A New Tale of the Genii*. Julia Curtis says it was by "an unnamed Charlestonian."[3] It is described in the published text as a masque and is inscribed to Thomas Jefferson, "President of the United States."

This masque allegorically tells of America's revolt against Britain's tyranny at the urging of France. It also warns against the continuing danger from Great Britain after the Revolution. In a dialogue of Elutheria (The Spirit of Liberty) with Americana in the first act, the former says she forsook the British shores. Elutheria says that previously she had pitied all nations but Britannia, who had possessed her. Britannia, however, rejected her. Americana promises that she will not cast Elutheria off. The fifth act contains a description of Galiana (France) and Americana going to war against the tyranny of Britannia in the Revolutionary War. In the final scene Galiana and Americana stand before Elutheria. Galiana asks Americana "Does this wide world contain two friends of freedom;/More just more faithful than thyself and me?"[4]

A newspaper reviewer in Charleston reported of *Americana* that "the general applause bestowed on this its first representation is a proof of its intrinsic merit."[5] Placide took a part in the production.[6] This masque is a good example of the kind of patriotic spectacle being put on in Charleston during the time of the French popularity in acting and politics.

Following these pro-Republican works came a play expressing Federalist views. *Liberty in Louisiana*, celebrating the Louisiana Purchase of 1803, was performed at the Charleston Theatre on April 4, 6, and May 21, 1804, and published in that year. It was by James Workman, a Federalist.[7] Workman had come to Charleston a few years before 1804, and had formed an association with the Federalist *Courier*. He later moved to New Orleans, where he became Judge of the County of Orleans from 1805 to 1807. He was active in the civic affairs of that city. As secretary for the Legislative Council of the Territory, he was responsible for much of the first legislation passed. In 1807 he was accused, but acquitted, of organizing an invasion of Mexico in connection with the notorious Burr Conspiracy.[8] He was the author of several published works.[9] In a collection of his earlier writings, *Politcial Essays* (1801), he had proposed an invasion of Spanish America, a common scheme of the time, and had expressed many sentiments that were to be repeated in *Liberty in Louisiana*.

Workman's play was widely seen and read. After the first performances at the Charleston Theatre in 1804, the play was presented in New York and Philadelphia during the same year and in Savannah in 1805.[10] In Charleston, criticism appeared in two newspapers: the *Times* and the *Courier*. The former, on April 9, 1804, noted the laughter of the audience and reported that leading actor John Hodgkinson gave as "animated a picture of the character of O'Flinn," a comic character, as the best performer on the British stage could offer. The *Courier* gave the greatest coverage to the play. S. C. Carpenter reviewed the play April 4, 1804, and again on April 19, 1804. He praised the play highly in his second review, but noted some grumblings from the audience because of the portrayals of an Irishman, a Scotsman, and a New Englander as "knaves." His answer was that "a knave" as well as an honest man is to be found in every country. He asserted that the object in view, "the commemoration of the introduction of the blessings of liberty into Louisiana," would cast respect upon "the piece, even if it had been what a few prejudicial critics have said of it." Since the play is Federalist in sympathy, the opposition may have come from Republicans in the audience.

This play depicts conditions in Louisiana at the time of the cession, expresses a widely held antagonism toward Spain, and presents a happy merging of the Franco-Spanish and American cultures. It is a particularly clear example of how the stage was used for political purposes in America at this time. Workman's first political objective is to denounce Spanish colonial rule, particularly the legal order, and thus to present the new American sovereignty as all the more glorious and desirable. There was a pressing need to win approval of the American government in 1804, since the inhabitants of Louisiana objected to many changes brought by the Americans, especially the new judicial system.[11] Workman's second aim was to express his Federalist opinions.

In the preface, Workman stated his purpose in composing this comedy. At first, he had thought of writing a political pamphlet, but after considering how sentiments embodied in a character or story can produce a superior effect, "with the splendor of theatrical decoration," he decided on a play as "the engine of enforcing his political opinions." He wrote in order to convey to the people of Louisiana the advantages they would derive from becoming part of the United States, "by illustrating the great principles of general and genuine liberty, and holding up despotism to alternate derision and abhorrence."[12]

Workman denounces "despotism" primarily through a satirical attack on the Spanish legal system in Louisiana. Although this theme pervades the whole comedy in the portrayal of the corrupt judge, it is emphasized most strongly in Act IV, Scene 2, when Don Bertholdo delivers as many decisions as possible at his last "audience," that is, session of court. The cases are heard privately and are presented by a "Scrivano," according to the Spanish system. The most ludicrous case concerns the bringing of contraband into the province by a New England trader, whose ship is anchored in the river. Smuggling in Louisiana was common at this time, and bribery of Spanish officials to permit it was notorious.[13] The New Englander Fairtrade protests that he is only carrying "a few onions and other small notions." Don Bertholdo replies that if he finds a single contraband article, he will throw him in chains for seven years. When Fairtrade offers a bribe of butter and cheese, he finds that the judge is only interested in money. Fairtrade offers him a copper coin, but Don Bertholdo says that all metals except gold are "porous" to him. Finally, Fairtrade gives him two doubloons after sighing, "The whale that swallowed Jonas was not half so voracious." The Yankee trader has the last laugh, nevertheless, when Don Bertholdo discovers after the smuggler has gone that the gold pieces are in fact "cased dollars," that is, have only a gold covering.

At the end of the drama, the hero, Captain O'Brien, an Irish gentleman in the American service, brings Don Bertholdo before the American general and accuses him of trying to carry off a local Spanish beauty, Laura, to Havana. Because of his high rank Don Bertholdo demands that Laura be awarded to him, but the general says that she is mature enough to act independently. Laura spurns Don Bertholdo, Workman's comic embodiment of Spanish misrule, and chooses the Irishman and life in Louisiana under American administration. The message is clear. The inhabitants of Louisiana, Spain's former colony, should unite with settlers from the United States under the aegis of American law.

Workman's purpose of supporting the Federalists can be seen clearly. He states on the dedication page that he inscribes the play to Chief Justice John Marshall, who has shown "kindness and favorable regard" to him. Marshall was a Federalist and a bitter enemy of Jefferson, the Republican president. Throughout the play, the attitude of some Republicans toward the law is satirized. The principal comic character, Phelim O'Flinn, an Irishman, represents the Republican viewpoint. He expresses views that Workman wishes to condemn. Phelim declares that the American law "never was fond of me, and I wish the devil had it and every other law in the world into the bargain" (I.i.). In reference to the repeal of the Judiciary Act by the Republicans, Phelim says that if Congress, instead of turning out a few "Judges awhile ago," had sent all "the blackguards about their business," a man might live "in peace and security, help himself to whatever he fancied, and leather any one he lik'd" (I.i.). Later in speaking of his marriage, Phelim describes the form of government that would suit him. He will not call his bride-to-be his sovereign because the country is soon to become a republic. Under that form of government, the president will do better "without either congress, judge or jury to impeach or bother you" (III.i).

Workman also satirizes the Republican position on the naturalization of citizens. Phelim remarks that after being in America five years you become a native, "and good luck to the brave boys that so ginerously [sic] share their noble privileges with strangers" (II.i). The Republicans had repealed a Federalist law which had increased the time necessary for naturalization from five to fourteen years. The requirement was only five years when Workman composed his play.[14] Workman thus attacks Republican actions through Phelim's comic statements. The pro-British attitude among Federalists is expressed by Workman when Phelim and his friends, Sawney, and Theresa, toast "the sister nations" of America, England, Ireland, and Scotland (II.i).

The Female Enthusiast, published in 1807, is an anti-French play by an anonymous author.[15] It is not known if this play was offered to the theatre, but it was not performed there. No play that was opposed to the Republican admiration for the French Revolution appeared during Placide's management at the Charleston Theatre. This play extols Charlotte Corday. She denounces the excesses of the French Revolution before murdering Marat. Marat is presented as a destructive radical. He shouts to the people:

Frenchmen! Countrymen! My brethren! be free
Stain your swords with the purple tide, flowing

From dying conspirators: let the foes
Of our liberty bleed—they are vipers.   (III.i)

Chabot tells Charlotte she is a "mad Enthusiast" whom France will condemn to the guillotine. She replies that if such is her doom, France is "the fetter'd slave" of "blood-thirsty men" (IV.ii). Duval speaks the author's viewpoint when he says that "this hated, monstrous revolution" makes our children as disobedient to the natural government of parents as to "the good old Regime of France" (III.iii).

The change from the politically partisan writing of the Federalist-Republican period to the non-partisan drama afterwards is clearly apparent in the next dramatist. The versatile Isaac Harby (1788-1828) achieved a measure of fame as a school teacher, journalist, dramatic critic, dramatist, and religious leader.[16] With a keen concern for the drama of his city and a thorough acquaintance with the classics and Shakespeare, he was qualified to write knowledgeable opinions on the drama. As a friend of Charles Gilfert's and a leading drama critic in Charleston, Harby is the best example of the close link between the author and local theatre which distinguished drama in Charleston during its flourishing years.

Harby's work with the public press was an important part of his career. In 1807 he began editing the *Quiver*, a weekly periodical. He next purchased *The Investigator*, changed its name to the *Southern Patriot*, increased its circulation, edited it as an organ expressing strong Republican sentiments, and supported the administration of James Madison. Harby was a vigorous supporter of the Republican Party, but his plays are not politically controversial. Other newspapers employing his talents were the *City Gazette* and the *Mercury*.[17]

Harby was a leader in the Jewish Reform Movement in America. Along with others in Charleston favoring change, he formed a new congregation in 1824 called "The Reformed Society of Israelites." His biographer, L. C. Moise, considers that in his work as a religious

MURAL OF PERSONALITIES CONNECTED WITH THE CHARLESTON
THEATRES, IN THE FOOTLIGHT PLAYERS WORKSHOP, CHARLESTON.
COURTESY, EMMETT ROBINSON. CONJECTURAL LIKENESSES ARE INDICATED BY*.

1. Monimia* (actress, 1735) 2. Mrs. Whitlock (English actress, Old Charleston Theatre) 3. Matthew Sully (actor, Old Charleston Theatre) 4. Henry Placide (comedian, son of Alexander) 5. Junius Brutus Booth 6. Edmund Kean 7. Fanny Essler 8. Charles Macready 9. Edwin Booth 10. Julia Dean (first appearance, 1852) 11. Joseph Jefferson 12. Otis Skinner 13. William Ioor* 14. John Blake White 15. Isaac Harby* 16. Mordecai Noah (dramatist) 17. Edwin Clifford Holland* 18. William Crafts* 19. William Gilmore Simms 20. Du Bose Heyward (after a painting by Alfred Hutty) 21. Alexander Placide* 22. Charles Gilfert* 23. "Thespis" (pseudonym of Stephen Cullen Carpenter)* 24. Dr. John Beaufain Irving

leader "lies the most important and the most abiding work of his useful life."[18] In June, 1828, Harby moved from Charleston to New York, where he established a connection with the *Evening Post*, a position in which, according to Simms, he maintained his fidelity to the "litterateurs" and press gang in Charleston.[19] He died in New York on December 14, 1828.

Harby's interest in the drama is well demonstrated by the fact that he wrote three plays as well as a considerable amount of dramatic criticism. His first play, "Alexander Severus," was turned down by Placide and never published. His next, *The Gordian Knot*, written in 1807, was not produced on the Charleston stage until May 3 and 10, 1810. His last play, *Alberti*, was presented by Gilfert on April 27 and 30, 1819. These works, unfortunately, do not possess sufficient artistry to offset their lack of a significant connection with contemporary life.

Harby's criticism received praise from his contemporaries. Simms noted that Harby was considered an able dramatic and literary critic who wrote essays and orations "with spirit, grace, and effect."[20] Abraham Moise, who published "A Memoir" along with a selection of Harby's writings in 1829, wrote that his general acquaintance with dramatic works and especially those of Shakespeare made him "a correct and severe judge of the proper conceptions of an actor." Sometimes his discovery of an error could severely affect the reputation of a performer.[21]

The selection of Harby's writings contains examples of his dramatic criticism. In his "Defence of the Drama" he emphasizes the theatre's role in improving society. It is as "a moral lever that the statesman and philosopher should regard the stage."[22] In his essay "The Merchant of Venice" he made a rare attack on his idol, Shakespeare, who bowed "to the prejudices of his age" in characterizing Shylock. He went on to say that we can still enjoy "the brilliancy" of the greatest poet of any age in spite of various objections to this play.[23] Other essays in this volume deal with famous actors in Charleston: Thomas A. Cooper as Othello and Coriolanus;

and Edmund Kean as Othello, Sir Giles Overreach, and Lear.

Harby's ideas about the drama were not restricted to the plays of Shakespeare and the performances of great actors, but included opinions about contemporary plays and his own compositions. He is most significant perhaps as a drama critic who applied his theories to his own plays. In fact, he is one of the leading representatives of the critic-playwright in this early period of American drama.

The first principle that governed the writing of Harby's plays was the rejection of the Gothic in favor of an imitation of nature. On this point, Harby was in company with American critics of romantic poetry because they too asked for an adherence to reality and insisted on probability. They objected to Gothic "wonders, and miracles, and supernaturalism" and were pleased to find the "glow of humanity and the solidity of real people in their romance, however ancient or faraway the scene."[24]

Harby stated his position against the Gothic melodrama most forcibly in his preface to *The Gordian Knot*. He explained how he had dealt with the "horrors" which appeared in the source for his play. His own composition was adapted from William Ireland's *Abbess*, a novel which in turn had its grounds in *Secreto Maligno* by an unknown Italian novelist. With the addition of "midnight assassinations" and "horrors," Ireland had fashioned "his terrible story in the true spirit of Germanic romance." Harby states that he took the main scenes in his first two acts from Ireland's novel, but no more. As for the rest of the play, Harby asserts that he proceeded on his own. "In pursuing NATURE, I found my road to be widely different from the path followed by Mr. Ireland." In fact, the novel served as a warning to shun its "monstrosities," and "by reasoning diametrically opposite to it, and making the motives and notions of my characters, to contrast it in every point, I generally gained in an adverse ratio, a nearer approach to truth."[25] Harby, thus, stresses the familiar principle that truth is to be found in following nature.

A writer to the Charleston *Times*, calling himself "Lucius," lamented the lack of public support given *The Gordian Knot*. It is the duty of the public, he wrote, "to receive favorably the *first* offerings of their youth." As a beginning work, the play merits "protection," and since it comes from one who has shown possession of *"eminent abilities*, it is entitled to *public favor.*" An overflowing house for the second performance would atone for "the neglect, not to say the contempt, that has attended the Play of Mr. Harby" (May 11, 1810).

Alberti is an improvement over *The Gordian Knot* since the plot, though typically intricate, is better handled and the revenge theme is developed more interestingly.[26] The setting is approximately that of the preceding play: Florence in 1480 during the rule of Lorenzo de Medici. The plot deals with the relinquishment of revenge by Alberti, a military hero just returning from battle as the play opens. Alberti forbids his son Ippolito, to marry Antonia, the daughter of his brother, Ridolpho, because he says that Ippolito is Ridolpho's son. The young couple are hence brother and sister. Filippo, the old servant, has a different story to tell. When Ridolpho's son, Cesario, died, Filippo replaced him with Alberti's son. Thus, when Alberti tried to take revenge on his brother for marrying the woman he had loved by stealing Cesario, he was in fact kidnapping his own son. Alberti, at last, abandons his desire for revenge on Ridolpho. He declares that he is glad to return a noble young man to his brother. The way is then open for the marriage of Ippolito and Antonia, whose kinship is only that of first cousins.

Like other contemporary plays with foreign settings, *Alberti* contains incidental sentiments applicable to American politics. Both Alberti and Lorenzo, the good ruler of republican Florence, praise republics and political independence. Alberti remarks that some men wrongly contend that republics are but anarchies, "rebellious/ Gainst right-divine" (II.i). Lorenzo declares that if tyranny were planted in Florence, he would cross the Atlantic to find "some wild retreat / and there court Independence" (V.i). The latter statement, even though it would have preceded Columbus's voyage by twelve years, must have pleased President James Monroe, who was present at the second performance of *Alberti*.

Alberti enjoyed more success with the public than *The Gordian Knot*. A writer for the *Southern Patriot* on April 28, 1819, reported on the first performance. The play went off with "eclat" and fulfilled the expectations "entertained from the talents of the author." The audience bestowed on the piece its flattering approval. Especially deserving of praise was the visiting star, Mr. Cleary, who played the role of Alberti "with great judgement and spirit." On April 30, 1819, the writer of a "Communication" to the *Southern Patriot* stated that *Alberti* would be offered for the author's benefit that evening and that "a bumper" was anticipated. The following day it was noted in the *Southern Patriot* that despite the warm weather, many attended *Alberti* with the president (May 1, 1819). On May 6, 1819, an announcement in the *Courier* stated that subscriptions would be taken at its office for the printing of *Alberti*.

Harby's experiences with the management of the Charleston Theatre provide an interesting view of author-manager relations during this period of dramatic writing. Fortunately he has left a vivid account of his attempts to get his first two plays produced by Placide. He had found encouragement to compose plays in the success of William Ioor and John Blake White. In 1806 he wrote of the hopes he had for his first drama, "Alexander Severus": "I was buoyed up in my laborious task . . . by the belief of its running the same chance of success that 'The Mystery of the Castle,' 'The Battle of Eutaw Springs,' & did."[27] These expectations were thwarted by "ALEXANDER PLACIDE, the manager, to *whom, I* was necessitated to submit." Placide told him the play lacked the incidents, "de something to catch de people." Placide had indeed been concerned with popular appeal from the days of his patriotic spectacles in the 1790's. The manager concluded his comments with praise for the tragedy as "a virgin performance" and with the advice that Harby should in his next attempt include more adventures and write better English. Harby particularly resented the latter comment since it came from a Frenchman speaking broken English. His difficulties with Placide were not over since the manager was slow in approving his second play for production. Referring to this next encounter Harby wrote: "How he then treated me we shall see hereafter."[28] Placide found defects which required cutting and recasting. Harby wrote that since Placide was not learned in English nor in English authors "the manner of his critiques no less than the matter, (like some innocent experiments in chemistry) were amusing rather than instructive."[29]

Willam Bulloch Maxwell (1787-1814) of Savannah, Georgia, tried unsuccessfully to have his single play accepted for production by Placide. Isaac Harby discussed this incident in a review of Maxwell's *The Mysterious Father* for his newspaper *The Quiver.* Maxwell, the first native of Georgia to compose a play, published his *The Mysterious Father* in 1807 in Savannah.[30] The play includes this democratic sentiment:

Mankind were all by nature equal made;
Men make themselves suspicious by deeds.   (IV.ii)

In his history of the Savannah theatre J. Max Patrick mentions that Maxwell may have seen plays in Charleston. Certainly he would have attended performances by the Charleston Company in Savannah; Placide regularly visited the Georgia city until the year 1805.[31] In his review of the printed edition of *The Mysterious Father*, Harby makes clear that Maxwell must have known of the beginnings of playwriting in Charleston. He wrote in his newspaper, *The Quiver*, that the support given to "our native productions, affords an opening prospect to future attempts. Encouraged by this anticipated view, a youth of Georgia has stepped forth on the stage. . . . "[32] The success of Ioor's and White's plays, thus, induced Maxwell to try playwriting also.

Harby mixed praises and criticism in his review of *The Myste-rious Father*. He observed in the character Pirozzi "a management and display of human feeling that are not unworthy the pen of a master bard." Concerning versification, Harby remarked that "the verse of Mr. Maxwell possesses a character of ease, with the softest harmony. The ear is sweetly impressed at the end of every line by the sounds of a melodious and diversified cadence." He does not approve of Maxwell's practice, common among dramatists, of con-cluding each act with rhyme, which "produces a wrong effect in tragedy, as the emotion raised by rhyme is dissonant to the sol-emnity of this species of composition."[33] Pirozzi, for example, ends Act IV with this judgment of the false monk's influence on Count Veroni:

> Although the vicious, for a transient while,
> May wear, all-prideful, exultations smile;
> Not long their fancy'd pleasures will endure,
> For virtue's triumph is, at last, secure.

Harby did not demand that Maxwell adhere strictly to the unities. He believed that only the unity of action need be maintained in tragedy and that Dryden and others were mistaken in their reve-rence for the rules of Bossu, the seventeenth century French critic. Maxwell, in fact, deserved blame for not slighting the unity of time and place, "when he might have amply compensated for it by embodying in his piece more of that interest which awakens curio-sity, and fixes attention." Harby finished his review, which was ob-viously meant to lessen Maxwell's disappointment over the rejection of his play, with an attack on Placide. This "theatrical carver for the public taste in Charleston" offers insignificant plays and harle-quinades "while the soft and sentimental efforts of Maxwell are hindered from their proper sphere of exhibition!"[34]

Edwin C. Holland (1794-1824) employed his poetic talent, which had already been demonstrated in his *Odes, Naval Songs and Other Occasional Poems* (1814),[35] to adapt Byron's *Corsair* especially for the Charleston Theatre. By profession a lawyer, Holland became editor of the Charleston *Times* in 1818. Simms described him as a pamphleteer who was involved in controversies, especially religious.[36] In 1822, he engaged in political debate when he published a pamphlet called "Refutation of the Calumies Circulated Against the Southern and Western states Respecting the Institution and Existence of Slavery."[37] Holland's relationship with Gilfert and his father-in-law, Joseph G. Holman, is clearly shown by his dramatic adaptation in blank verse of *The Corsair*, originally in rhymed couplets. Music for the piece was composed by Gilfert himself and was dedicated by Holland to Holman, whose "critical and discriminating judgement" would have made this piece "more acceptable to public taste."[38] Holland's and Gilfert's melodrama about Lord Conrad opens with a chorus of pirates and ends with a "Solemn Requiem."

The Corsair was first performed on February 18, 1818, and afterwards on February 20 and 21, 1818. A writer for the *City Gazette and Commercial Daily Advertiser* on February 20, 1818, reported that the audience at the first performance of *The Corsair* was numerous and respectable. In scenic effect and music, the taste of the manager and artist were well displayed. Referring to the author, this correspondent stated that "Mr. H." was well known "and his literary talents have often come under public inspection." The public will now decide if "native genius is to be encouraged or neglected." He emphasized that the wishes of his newspaper were warmly in the author's favor.

Charles Gilfert must have felt honored that William Crafts decided to write a dramatic work, *The Sea-Serpent,* for his company. William Crafts (1787-1826), poet, essayist, and orator, was the most prominent literary figure of Charleston during this period and a fervent Federalist. Slight though his literary accomplishments were, they established his reputation in Charleston. William P. Trent comments that Crafts was for many years the "literary dictator of Charleston." He had a particular interest in the theatre during the "golden days of the drama in Charleston"[39] and came to its defense in a witty essay pointing out the revenue which the city received from taxing this institution.[40]

Crafts was born in Charleston, the son of a Boston merchant. In 1805, he graduated from Harvard and returned to Charleston, where he became a lawyer and member of the legislature. In 1821, he became editor of the *Courier* and contributed to it a literary quality.[41] Shortly after being admitted to the bar in 1809, Crafts identified himself with the Federalists. J. B. O'Neall writes that Crafts "adhered to their principles to the day of his death, with the constancy of a martyr." The barriers of party obstructed Crafts' advancement before the War of 1812, O'Neall observes, "for Mr. Crafts was a Federalist, and in opposition to the war measures, and this often stood in his way."[42]

Though Crafts reveals some romantic influences in his poetry —for example, by his imitation of Thomas Moore's Anacreontic poems—he does not stray far from the neo-classic style. V. L. Parrington states that Crafts and Robert Treat Paine marked the "last ebbing of the eighteenth century before the wit ideal was submerged by the incoming tide of romanticism."[43] With the exception of Byron and Moore, the Romantic poets made little impression on him. His "Sullivan's Island" is in the manner of "Windsor Forest"; "The Raciad," an account of the Race Week in Charleston, is in the vein of *The Rape of the Lock.*[44] The latter poem is satirical and in heroic couplets. *A Selection, in Prose and Poetry; from the Miscellaneous Writings of the late William Crafts* was published after his death in 1828.

Crafts' *Sea-Serpent*[45] is a satirical drama written in heroic couplets. It derides a contemporary event, the discovery of a fish in Massachusetts that was first thought to be a sea-serpent. O'Neall describes Crafts' treatment of this incident: "About the time of the advent of the sea-seprent, he wrote a *jeu d'esprit* in dramatic verse, upon this topic, which had at the time considerable celebrity."[46]

In a humorous essay called "Charleston," in which he requests travelers to report any information of interest they have gathered, Crafts writes, "Can you furnish any additional evidence of the Sea Serpent?"[47]

This play concerns the gullibility of those who speculated on the existence of a monster which some sailors claimed to have seen near Gloucester, Massachusetts. The public officials of Gloucester and the scientists of Boston are greatly interested in this news. The Justice and Mayor of Gloucester envision the fame that will come to their city. The Justice declares:

> Let Salem boast her museum, and her witches,
> Her statues Newb'ry, Marblehead her riches—
> We from them all the shining now will take,
> The snake and Glo'ster, Glo'ster and the snake!

The Mayor dispatches an attendant to the state capital immediately:

> To Boston, famous for its men of sense,
> Post we immediate this intelligence.
> Go tell the Parsons that the Devil's caught,
> 'Twill save them much of preaching and of thought.   (I.iv)

Tom Codus, a comic servant, tells his sweetheart, Molly, that he will catch the monster and make a fortune from it, which they can enjoy after their marriage. Tom returns with the creature, which turns out to be disappointingly small. According to the stage directions, some men enter "bringing a Horse-Mackeral" or some fish as much like a snake as can "conveniently be procured" (III.ii). The Boston scientist, who bears the famous name of "Linnaeus," states the moral at the end of the play: Replace credulity with "sober common sense."

A satire of New England would not have been complete without a comment on the Yankee's travels. Tom Codus remarks to a group of Yankee sailors:

One cannot go
To a bleak rock, or barren waste of snow
A burning mountain or an arid sand
But sees a yankee soon as he sees land.   (III.ii)

The Sea-Serpent was given as an after-piece on May 12, 1819,
and after *Hamlet,* again on May 2, 1821. It was performed in
Richmond on July 4, 1820, as a "satirical burlesque," by Gilfert's
company, which at this time played a season at the Richmond
Theatre.[48] "Dramaticus" wrote in the Charleston *City Gazette* for
May 12, 1819, that from the title "The Sea Serpent, or Gloucester
Hoax," theatre-goers may expect something witty. He has pursued
the work and assures them they will not be disappointed. He trusts
that the citizens will patronize this play "and keep up their National
character—it is written by a gentleman of this city." Writing in the
Southern Patriot on the same day, "Momus" was glad that this
"native production," *The Sea-Serpent*, was to be performed for the
first time. Besides humor and poetry, it would afford pleasure since
it was a benefit for the author. Simms called this *jeu d'esprit* "an
elaborate joke, lively with occasional hits, social, political, and
moral."[49]

James Wright Simmons (c. 1790-1858) composed four plays.
They were *Manfredi, Valdemar; or The Castle of the Cliff, The
Master of Ravenswood,* and *De Montalt, or The Abbey of St. Clair.*
The first two were printed but not performed.[50] The third and
fourth were presented April 12, 1824, and February 2, 1843, re-
spectively, at the Charleston Theatre, but not printed. Simmons
was co-editor with Simms of a magazine called the *Southern
Literary Gazette* and one of his closest friends. At one time, he
worked for the New York *Mirror* and the New York *Courier.*
Later he went West and became comptroller general and treasurer
of the Republic of Texas. Simms evaluated his verse and prose in
the *Magnolia.* He stated that though much might be found "ob-
jectionable in various points of view," there was "enough highly

charged with original thought and fancy, and highly beautiful in expression, to place him conspicuous in the catalogue of American writers."[51]

Maria Henrietta Pinckney published three plays in a collection called *Essays, Religious, Moral, Dramatic and Poetical* in 1818.[52] Though not performed, they illustrate the popularity of dramatic writing in Charleston at this time. Miss Pinckney was the daughter of General Charles Cotesworth Pinckney, Federalist candidate for president in 1804 and 1808. Of the three plays in her collection the first is most interesting, *The Young Carolinians; or, Americans in Algiers.* It is a patriotic drama expressing sympathy for Americans imprisoned by Algerian pirates. Since the Barbary Wars extended from 1785 to 1816, this play was probably written some years before its publication. The play alternates between settings abroad and at home. It presents an interesting contrast between two elderly persons: Miss Woodberry, a lady of low-country high society, and "Homespun," a man from the backcountry. Also it contains a Negro character, the first to appear in a play by a South Carolinian. "Cudjo" delivers a defense of slavery:

> To be sure I slave for true; but poor folks must work everywhere. Suppose me poor buckra; well, I serve some rich buckra, him pay me; but when Cudjo sick, or lame, or old too much for work, him turn me away; now misses give me too much nasty stuff for cure me—plenty sweet tea to wash em down;—bye and bye get well again, she look pon me with one kind eye, same like a dove— glad to see poor old Cudjo well.   (IV.iii)

Maria Pinckney anticipated subsequent Southern authors by having a slave defend slavery. Simms, for example, presents Tom, a slave in *Woodcraft*, arguing in favor of the institution.[53]

From 1797 to 1825, dramatic writing in Charleston demonstrated the shift from controversial political plays of the Federalist-Republican period to the non-partisan plays of the Era of Good

Feeling. The large number of plays published and performed exhibits the popularity of dramatic writing at this time.

1826 to the Civil War

From 1826 to the Civil War, following the best period of playwriting for the Charleston theatre, there continued to be the composition of plays, but fewer were produced. The theatre became more a place of pure entertainment and less a patron of plays written by local writers. There are a number of causes for this change. The theatre was less of an independent, local institution because of the reliance on stars and traveling entertainment; there was often an avoidance of controversial topics; and there was a turning to the novel as the main vehicle of literary expression as seen in the career of Simms.

Contemporary observers lamented the lack of original dramatic writing. In 1829, a writer for the *Southern Literary Gazette*, published in Charleston, stated that there was no good dramatic writing being done. Audiences did not support the theatre as they should. These conditions were unfortunate because the theatre could serve as a strong moral force. He gave as an example a play by John Blake White formerly produced in Charleston. He commended his *Modern Honor* for attacking "the disgraceful practice of Duelling."[54] In 1852, Simms gave an explanation for the dearth of dramatic composition when he was trying to get his play, *Norman Maurice*, produced at the Charleston Theatre. He wrote the manager, Francis Colburn Adams, that he had found no encouragement to write plays because of the poor condition of the theatre. He stated that the theatre had been "kept down" by the actors themselves "who are generally unwilling to study new parts and do justice to them."[55] On the rare occasion of a local play at the Charleston Theatre, there was enthusiastic praise. In 1843, a reviewer of "Theatricals" in the *Magnolia, or Southern Apalachian*, which was edited by Simms, welcomed the appearance of plays by

Charlestonians. He said that the manager (who was then W. C. Forbes) seemed bent on "the only policy which can revive the theatre—the introduction of new pieces." In the current season, he noted "De Montalt" by James W. Simmons and "The Battle of Fort Moultrie" by another "gentleman of Charleston."[56]

The number of plays written by South Carolinians but not produced for the theatre illustrates the continued urge to write plays. John Blake White's *The Forgers*, (composed in 1828 and published in 1837) was not performed. *Norman Maurice*, which Simms considered his best play, met the same fate. Moreover, several plays by Simms remained in manuscript, like *Timon of Athens* and *Don Carlos;* his *Benedict Arnold* was finally published during the Civil War but never performed. Mrs. Louisa S. M'Cord (1810–1877), a well-known contributor to such magazines as the *Southern Quarterly Review, Debow's Review,* and the *Southern Literary Messenger,* published a closet drama, *Caius Gracchus,* in 1851. William Elliott (1788-1863) of Beaufort, known for his *Carolina Sports by Land and Water* (Charleston, 1846), published a blank verse tragedy, *Fiesco,* in 1850.

During this period there is evidence of distaste for political plays in the South. James H. Dormon in *Theatre in the Ante Bellum South, 1815–1861,* discusses the avoidance of political topics. He quotes a letter to the *Courier,* December 4, 1827, in which the correspondent asks that "the Manager positively forbid *politics"* on the stage. Jackson and Adams make up our breakfasts, dinners and suppers. For God's sake, let us be amused with something else when we 'go . . . to the play.'" Dormon states that "political agitation" was a sure means of reducing theatre audiences in the period.[57]

Despite some dislike of politics on the stage from 1825 to the Civil War, a considerable number of political subjects reached the American stage, North and South. The struggle between Whigs and Democrats appeared in the pro-Whig play *Whigs and Democrats, or Love of No Politics* (published in Richmond anonymously, 1839, and performed in Philadelphia in that year).[58] Disputes over the territories, Oregon, California, and Texas, and battles of the Mexican War were also treated in plays. Overshadowing all other subjects in the course of time was slavery. Soon after Harriet Beecher Stowe's *Uncle Tom's Cabin* was published in 1852, dramatic versions began to appear. The first successful one was by George L. Aiken, first played in September,1852. It opened later in New York, July 18, 1853 and was performed over two hundred times successively, lasting until April 19, 1854, an unprecedented run.[59] Other anti-slavery plays were *Dred,* a dramatization of Mrs. Stowe's second novel of slavery (first produced September 22, 1856), and Dion Boucicault's poignant *The Octoroon* (1859).[60]

Uncle Tom's Cabin was not welcome in the South. The farthest south it came was to Baltimore in 1855 and St. Louis in 1858. A spate of Southern rebuttals, however, appeared. There were Irish burlesques in New Orleans, and in Charleston a burlesque version was played by Kunkel's Troupe October 24–26, 1853. There are no extant copies of these parodies but the version in Charleston was described in the newspaper as showing the "real history of a fugitive, who, weary of living free to starve among abolition bigots, returns voluntarily to slavery."[61]

Although the theatre in Charleston was not the political forum it had been, the following list shows that it still served from time to time as a political and patriotic platform. The plays extend from 1828 to 1861 and were often given on such holidays as Washington's birthday: *Battle of New Orleans,* January 8, 1828 (anniversary of the battle and given in the year that Jackson was first elected); *Hail Columbia,* February 22, 1834; *Siege of Charleston,* February 22, 23, 28, 1843; *Star Spangled Banner,* December 8, 9, 1843 ;*Columbus,* February 22, 1845; Simms's *Michael Bonham, or the Fall of Bexar,* celebrating the annexation of Texas and given for the benefit of the Calhoun Monument Association, March 26, 27, 28, 1855; and "A Grand Apotheosis to the Confederate States, The Past! The Present!! The Future!!!" on November 27, 1861.

Besides Simms in this period, Augustus Julian Requier (1825-

1887) deserves special attention since he wrote a play that was both produced and published. Requier's mother was a refugee from the slave insurrection in Santo Domingo in 1791 that had brought French theatrical talent to Charleston. His first play was *The Spanish Exile* (published anonymously in Charleston, 1844).[62] It was performed at the Charleston Theatre, March 28 and April 1, 1844. Requier studied law and was admitted to the Charleston bar in 1844. He lived for a time in Marion, South Carolina, where he was editor of the newspaper. In 1850 he settled in Mobile, and in 1853 President Franklin Pierce appointed him United States district attorney for Alabama. During the Civil War, Jefferson Davis appointed him district attorney for the Confederacy. In 1866 he moved to New York, where he was assistant district attorney. He was identified with the Democratic Party there and had an active interest in Tammany Hall. His writings include a prose narrative of colonial South Carolina, *The Old Sanctuary. A Romance of the Ashley* (Boston: Redding and Company, 1846); and *Poems* (Philadelphia: J. B. Lippincott, 1860). The latter contains a closet drama, *Marco Bozzaris. A Play in Three Acts.*[63]

The performance of Requier's *The Spanish Exile* illustrates again a close relationship of dramatist and manager at the Charleston Theatre and the support of the local press. The first performance of this play was chosen by W. C. Forbes for his benefit, March 28, 1844. It was then given for Requier's benefit on April 1, 1844. In the *Courier,* March 28, 1844, appeared the following notice under "The New Charleston Theatre": for this evening, "an original Drama, entitled The Spanish Exile, written by a gentleman of this city." The cast was as follows:

    Fernando .... Mr. Forbes
    Alberto .... [Mr.] Charles
    Eleonora .... Mrs. Forbes

On April 1, 1844, the *Courier,* printed a "Notice of the Theatre." It stated that Mr. Forbes had postponed his departure for Augusta. *The Spanish Exile* was to be presented that evening with the author in the role of "Alberto." It was a benefit for the author, "from whose talents we have great expectations." The editors trusted the "young author" would receive "substantial encouragement." Also in this issue of the *Courier* a correspondent wrote that *The Spanish Exile* would test the public's support of native genius. The city had always fostered such work with "a parental feeling." The author has through vicissitudes devoted himself to belles-lettres, and this correspondent believed he would soon hold a prominent place among American authors. He noted that the first representation of the play was a "success." It is interesting to note that Requier's play was performed at the very time that Simms's *Michael Bonham* was turned down. Perhaps Requier's play would act better or eschewed politics. As will be shown below, it was Simms who continued the tradition of the Charleston stage as a medium for arguing the most urgent issues of the day.

III

WILLIAM IOOR

William Ioor was the first native of South Carolina whose name we know to compose a play and was among the very first dramatists in the South. Robert Munford of Virginia holds best claim to first place. His two comedies were written before the Revolution and published in 1798, but so far as is known did not reach the stage.[1] Ioor, whose two plays were performed initially in 1805 and 1807, is the next dramatist of any note to appear in the South.

Ioor was born on January 4, 1780, in St. George's parish, near old Dorchester, South Carolina, and died in Greenville District, South Carolina, on July 30, 1850.[2] He was married to Ann Mathewes, a relative of the Revolutionary governor of South Carolina, John Mathews. The couple had nine children and many descendants, some of whom are living in the state today. According to family tradition, the Ioors were French Huguenots who were forced to flee to Holland, where they adopted the present Dutch spelling of the name. The following variations of the name have appeared: Joor, Jour, Yoor, and I'oor. The most common spelling is "Ioor," usually pronounced "yōr."

In 1714, the founders of William's line, Nicholas and Catherine, immigrated from Holland to South Carolina. John Ioor, the grandfather of William, received a land grant on the Ashley River in Berkeley County from King George III in 1762. He and John Ioor, Jr., the father of William, are buried in the cemetery of St. George's parish church. During the Revolutionary War, which William Ioor wished so fervently to commemorate, the Ioor name was well known. Captain Joseph Ioor, his uncle, served on the *Randolph,* which went down in a fight with a British frigate in 1778.[3]

Before 1800, while still quite young, Ioor received his diploma of medicine in Philadelphia. At the end of the eighteenth and beginning of the nineteenth century, many South Carolinians went to the University of Pennsylvania for medical training. Ioor returned to South Carolina and in 1805 and 1808 was listed as a physician in the Dorchester area.[4] In 1805, he gave his residence on the title page of his first play, *Independence,* as "St. George, Dorchester, South-Carolina," the same as his birthplace.[5]

During the years when Ioor began to practice medicine, he was also much concerned with politics. He served as a member of the General Assembly from St. George, Dorchester, in the session 1800-1801 and 1802-1803.[6] This was the period of Jefferson's administration, the rise of the Republican Party in South Carolina, and the beginning tension with Great Britain over America's neutral rights during the Napoleonic Wars. Ioor turned to the theatre as a platform for his political views. *Independence,* which was performed on March 30, April 1, 1805, and February 26, 1806, praises the economic and intellectual independence of the American farmer, the mainstay of the Republican Party, while ostensibly presenting a comedy of English rural life. Ioor's second play, *The Battle of Eutaw Springs,* advocates a strong stand against Great Britain.[7] More widely seen than *Independence,* it was acted first for three nights in the 1806–07 season of the Charleston Theatre on January 10, 14, and February 23, 1807. An announcement in the *Courier* (January 13, 1807) stated that the performance on January 14 would be for the benefit of the author and that "an Epilogue by a Young Lady, will be spoken by Mr. Sully."[8] The play was repeated next season on May 9, 1808 and in Richmond on September 27, 1811, by the Charleston Theatre company, then managed by Alexander Placide.[9] It was given in Philadelphia on June 9, 1813, by the troupe of William Twaits, formerly associated with the Charleston Theatre.[10] The importance of these dramatic compositions in Ioor's life is indicated by the following statement in his obituary: "A short time prior to our last struggle with Great Britain, and while we were yet smarting under a sense of recently redressed wrongs, prompted by a spirit of patriotism, he wrote his two plays, 'The Battle of Eutaw Springs,' and 'Independence,' both of which were performed in Charleston."

Ioor's support of the small farmer in *Independence* indicates that he was engaged in farming in his rural parish, St. George's. It was common to find a combination of planter and physician in the small towns and rural districts. Dr. Samuel Cordes, who practised medicine in the parish of St. James, Santee, from about 1813 to 1850, also engaged in planting.[11]

The remaining facts available on Ioor's life may be given briefly. Sometime after his plays were presented, he moved to Savannah, Georgia, where he "practised Physic" for fifteen years "with eminent success," according to the obituary. In this change of residence Ioor was following a trend since after the Revolution many residents of Dorchester moved to Georgia and left the town to decay.[12] William Gilmore Simms recalled meeting Ioor on a deer hunt around 1830 and described his as a "cherry, humorous, old gentleman."[13] According to a story told among Ioor's descendants, Dr. Ioor was originally well-to-do, but being amiable and obliging had an unfortunate habit of lending money to friends. Many of these loans were never repaid and finally he suffered such reduced circumstances that he was unable to maintain his customary way of living in Charleston and moved to the up-country.

In the last part of his life, Dr. Ioor took up residence in Green-

HOME OF WILLIAM IOOR, NEAR PELZER, S.C.,
ON STATE HIGHWAY 8.
COURTESY, ELIZABETH MCDAVID.

ville District. He and his family had previously come to the area as summer residents, and his wife was a founder of Christ Church parish church,[14] built there in 1826.[15] The couple's names appear in the parish records now held by Christ Episcopal Church, Greenville. Ioor seems to have continued his medical practice after moving to this district. He died at his residence, which is still standing about a mile from Pelzer, South Carolina, and is buried beside his wife in the Springwood Cemetery, Greenville. His obituary ends, "The grief of a large circle of relatives and friends testified eloquently to his worth."

Independence

Two modern critics of *Independence* have failed to see its true significance.[16] Arthur Hobson Quinn called it "the first native play to treat English life with a real appreciation of its social values." Ludwig Lewisohn said that it was supposed to illustrate the effete character of the English nobility.[17] Its principle importance, however, is that *Independence* expresses ideas of Jeffersonian Republicanism, the most vital political philosophy at this time in America. Although its setting is England, *Independence* is concerned with American life and dramatizes the main belief uniting the various interest groups of the Jeffersonian Republican Party: independent farmers make the best citizens.[18] Ioor, in fact, by writing *Independence* joined the Federalist-Republican controversy that pervaded the poetry and drama of this era.

There is a good authority for calling *Independence* the first play of South Carolina. Ioor states in the preface to *Independence* that South Carolinians should "foster it, as it is the first play ever produced by a native of their state." S. C. Carpenter, editor and drama critic of the *Courier,* entitled his review of the play "The First Born of Carolina / Independence / A Comedy — by Dr. Joor." He wrote in the *Courier,* April 1, 1806, that this play was "the first by a native of Carolina, and the State has a right to be grateful to the author, who has afforded so fair an augury of their future drama."

The key to an understanding of Ioor's *Independence* is provided by the work on which it is based. Ioor states in the preface to *Independence* that it is adapted from the novel *The Independent,* and the reader is invited to consult that work to see "how much I am indebted" to the "anonimous [sic] author." The edition of this English novel, published in 1784, gives no author's name,[19] but it is now identified as being by Andrew McDonald.[20] A comparison of the novel and the play reveals, on one hand, that the plots are basically the same and that Ioor used large sections and many speeches in the novel with only a very few changes in wording. On the other hand, it is clear that Ioor omitted numerous parts, and added sentences, passages and scenes of his own.[21] Furthermore, he focused attention on the small independent farmer: his life, ideas, and virtues. His play, therefore, deserves to be considered a drama in its own right.

The plots of both works may be summarized together. Lord Fanfare, the dissolute owner of a large country estate, attempts to acquire the small farm of Charles Woodville. His offers to the farmer and the strategems of his lawyer, Whittington, all fail. Charles, helped out of financial embarrassment by Colonel Wynyard (Whynyard in the novel), who in the end reveals himself as his father, is triumphant and retains his farm. Subplots present the efforts of Woodville to gain the hand of Louisa Fanfare and those of Lord Fanfare to seduce the sister of Woodville, Lady Violet. Again, Woodville wins by humiliating the philandering lord in a mock-trial at a Gothic castle and by obtaining the hand of Louisa.

Changes made by Ioor show convincingly that he composed with the sentiments of his American audience in mind. The most striking evidence is a statement made by Colonel Wynyard when he is declaring how much he loves Louisa Fanfare. He says that he loves her "as well as all NATIVE AMERICANS love, the MEMORY of their WASHINGTON" (V.iii). Another interesting alteration shows a desire not to offend Catholics. Lord Fanfare appears at his masquerade in the novel as the Pope, but as Alexander the Great in the play.

More significant, however, is Ioor's whole shift of emphasis in the play. The stated purpose of the novel is to condemn "conjugal infidelity" (preface, p. v.). The play, on the other hand, aims primarily at a glorification of the farmer and his life in the country. In order to place emphasis on the farmer, Ioor, first, added a subtitle to his play: "Which Do You Like Best, the Peer, or the Farmer?" Next, he changed the epigraph. In the novel, three lines from Juvenal in Latin on the title page warn against sexual licentiousness and unrestrained passions. The quotation on the title page of Ioor's play is from James Thomson's *The Seasons* and is in praise of "the pure pleasure of country life."

Ioor's most important accomplishment in *Independence* is the dramatic portrayal of one of the most important and popular figures of this time: the small independent farmer. Farmers were powerful in American politics and made up the rank and file of the Republican Party. Furthermore, the farmer had been extolled by the great Republican himself, Jefferson, who, as well as many others, had written often of the farmer's independence. In his famous *Notes on Virginia*, the philosopher of agrarianism stated: "Cultivators of the earth are the most virtuous and independent citizens."[22] David Ramsay, in his *History of South-Carolina*, published in 1809, contrasted the large planters with the farmers by saying that the latter "depend more on their own exertions" and have "greater internal resources to meet extraordinary emergencies."[23] In *A View of South-Carolina*, printed in 1802, John Drayton recorded that "the middle and lower class of people," which would include the farmer, "possess a sufficient competence to make them independent, and a sufficient independence to render them happy."[24]

Charles Woodville, as characterized by Ioor, is independent in several significant ways. At the time Ioor wrote, in the post-Revolutionary period, indebtedness was the curse of many Americans. Woodville is free of debts, however. In the first act, when Fan-

fare approaches and tries to awe him as a man of quality, Woodville retorts, "Quality is no word of conjuration with me, I assure
you. I am an independent farmer, don't owe five guineas in the
world" (I.ii). The latter sentence is added in the play. Woodville
is also independent in that he supplies his own food and comforts.
Describing his farm in a remark not in the novel, Woodville says
that his farm yields "every necessary comfort for me and mine"
(I.ii). Thirdly, the hero of the play is independent in his thinking
and actions. He resists doggedly the threats and stratagems of Fanfare and Whittington to obtain his land. Talking with Lady Violet,
Woodville says that Lord Fanfare is covetous of gaining his farm,
but it does not accord with his "independent spirit to humor the
peer" (II.i). This statement and the whole scene with Lady Violet
were added by the dramatist.

Ioor sums up the farmer's independence from the land and money
of others in a statement not found in the novel. Fanfare's lawyer,
Whittington, reports that Woodville has a reputation for "boast-
ing of, his INDEPENDENCE, and declaring, that an honest farmer
knows of no dependence, except on heaven" (I.i). The reference to
"heaven" recalls a statement in *Notes on Virginia* (first published
1784-85). Jefferson scorns those depending for their subsistence
on "casualties and caprice of customers" instead of "looking up to
heaven, to their own soil and industry, as does the husbandman."[25]
Because of this similarity and others mentioned, it seems likely that
Notes on Virginia influenced Ioor in writing *Independence*.

Ioor has preserved fully the presentation of Woodville as a man
of high character. This characteristic bears out Jefferson's belief that
farmers are God's "peculiar deposit for substantial and genuine
virtue."[26] Woodville in his youth had surrendered to gambling and
to associating with bad companions, but he reformed, thanks to
Colonel Wynyard and rural life. He tells Louisa, quoting from
Hamlet's "To be, or not to be" soliloquy, that he knew "all the horrors of dependence, 'the whips and scorn of the time, the proud
man's contumely, and, the pangs of despised love'." In a talk with

the colonel, he resolved to change his ways and declared, "Farewell folly, glare, and deceit—welcome retirement, innocence, and INDEPENDENCE!" Since then has led the rural life in all its joys, "happy in my INDEPENDENCE, and resolute to maintain it" (I.v).

A common sentiment of the times is Woodville's Rousseauistic preference for rural over urban pleasures. In the play, he remarks that while sleeping in the shade of his trees he does not envy "your lordship's silken canopies; nor while laughing by my hall fire of a winter's night, do I sigh for the glare of an opera or a masquerade" (I.ii). And in the last act, Woodville declines to leave the country. He says in a soliloquy, "No, I will never quit my farm, but heighten every natural charm to a higher bloom." Ioor's sharpest satire of city snobbery comes in an expansion of Lady Fanfare's dialogue. Shocked to learn that Louisa grew up in the country, she calls it a sin and shame to rear a "decent female in the odious country!!!" (I.iii).

Ioor retains in his play the fact that Woodville is a great favorite with his workers and that he joins them in the fields. Roger, a farm hand, idolizes his master. Furthermore, when Woodville first appears, he is holding a hay rake and has been working alongside his men in the fields. This scene fits a contemporary description of the farmer in South Carolina. Ramsay notes that farmers have few or no slaves and when they own a few, "labor is performed jointly by whites and blacks."[27]

The portrait of the independent farmer given by Ioor is, of course, highly idealized, but as previously indicated there existed models in real life. Facts on the farmer of this time offer ample support. The farmer's independence in finances and in providing his own food and comforts is commented on at length by Lewis Cecil Gray in his *History of Agriculture in the Southern United States to 1860*. The small farmer incurred small expense, invested little capital, and took on no regular financial obligations. He differed from the larger planter in devoting his attention to general farming rather than to the production of rice and cotton, the great staples, and thus was self-sufficient. Sturdy independence and self-respect were his distinctive characteristics.[28] Jefferson believed that the farmer's independence of character was a direct outgrowth of economic independence.[29] In regard to his morals, they were judged to be high also, thus corroborating the appraisal of Jefferson. According to a report from North Carolina, the middle class planters were "honest, pious, and substantial."[30]

In addition to its praise of the farmer, Ioor's play illustrates very well another major rallying point of the Republicans, their hostility to Great Britain, and its corollary, their friendliness toward France. The depiction of Lord Fanfare as a ridiculous representative of the English nobility would appear to an American audience as anti-British in purpose. Ioor increased the anti-British tone by additions to the novel. After Woodville first meets the pompous Fanfare in his hay field in the first act, he says in an ironic aside, "What a hopeful situation would Old England be in, could she boast of many such peers of the realm, as the sample before us!" The anti-British nature of *Independence* was recognized by Ludwig Lewisohn, who wrote that Ioor satisfied the prejudices of his countrymen by making the English lord a silly monster.[31] Ioor reveals the pro-French sentiment of Republicans by changing Fanfare's valet in the novel, "La Fleche," a Frenchman who talks ludicrously broken English, to an Englishman named "Thomas."

A striking change made by Ioor is his handling of Fanfare's lawyer, Whittington. In both the novel and the play, he is the lord's accomplice in trying to seize Woodville's farm, and he buys up all the debts of Woodville's miller in order to take possession of the farmer's grain crop stored in the mill. Ioor, however, makes numerous and important additions to the lawyer's role. In the play, Whittington has definite plans to acquire Fanfare's estate, which he successfully carries out in the end. After a talk with Fanfare, the lawyer says in a soliloquy that if the peer will play a few more games of picquet and lose "a few more thousand guineas," he will

soon occupy the lord's "mansion house" (I.i). Ioor frequently ex-
pands the dialogue of Whittington. The lawyer's specific offer to
buy Woodville's farm for three thousand pounds and his warning
of how much it will cost to retain "eminent counsel" in court to
regain his grain are only in the play (IV.ii). Ioor also gives Whittington lines in a conversation with Fanfare which enable him to
satirize himself: "Damn the grand jury! no I ask the grand jury's
pardon, if it was not for them, the lord have mercy upon us honest
lawyers" (V.i).

By showing his dislike of lawyers, Ioor is expressing an attitude
found commonly among Republicans.[32] He is, moreover, reflecting
a general prejudice against the legal profession. Charles Warren
names as the first obstruction to the growth of the American Bar
from 1789 to 1815 the unpopularity of lawyers as a class. This attitude arose because the chief business of lawyers was the collection
of debts and the enforcement of contracts.[33] In South Carolina, lawyers were also disliked because of the large fees they obtained from
cases growing out of the Europan wars.[34]

Ioor's additions to the scenes when the villainous lawyer is present have a factual basis in the conditions of his own state and thus
indicate that frequently Ioor must have written with local conditions in mind. In the scene when Whittington confronts Woodville
with the news that his miller is bankrupt, Roger cries out that he
wishes "it would please the Lord to banish all the lawyers to
America." This remark appears also in the novel, but next Ioor
has Roger add that he has "heard say as how they've more there
already, than they know what to do with" (IV.1). Ramsay notes
especially the increase in the number of lawyers in South Carolina:
"The whole number admitted to the bar for the 27 years which immediately preceded the revolution was 58; but in the 25 years subsequent to its termination in 1783 no less than 238 were admitted
in Charleston, exclusive of those who passed their examination in
the country."[35] It is not possible to verify conclusively all the allusions that Ioor made to local conditions, but this one to lawyers is

clearly supported by contemporary evidence. We may assume that it was not missed at the Charleston Theatre.

Besides the lawyer, Ioor's principal object of satire is the peer, and much of the effectiveness of the play results from the striking contrast between this large landowner and the small farmer. Even when the haughty peer demands that Woodville sell his farm at their first meeting, the farmer offers him friendship if Fanfare will respect his independence. This contrast points up the concept of Jeffersonian Republicanism that farmers are the best members of society.

There is considerable evidence from the historical period to indicate that Ioor is in fact attacking the large planter of South Carolina, in addition to satirizing the English nobleman, by contrasting Fanfare with Woodville. Ramsay notes that "the farmer" had fewer vices and stronger character than "the planter."[36] Jefferson's sympathies were always with the small farmers of western Virginia and not with the great Tidewater planters, who aped the English squires.[37] Fanfare's attempt to acquire the small farm of Woodville is paralleled by the efforts of the rich to buy out the less wealthy planters and unite old homesteads into one vast estate in low-country South Carolina. By 1805 (the date of the production of *Independence*), the agriculture of low-country South Carolina had entered upon a program of large-scale production.[38] It appears probable that it was this very development that Ioor wished to attack in his play.

There are further striking similarities between the peer and the wealthy planter. The lord's large debt to Colonel Wynyard corresponds to the indebtedness of South Carolina planters, which Ramsay described as one of their principal faults.[39] Fanfare's extravagant living and immorality have a basis in the conduct of the aristocratic planters of South Carolina. Drayton wrote that "the richer part of the community" in South Carolina lived like that class in Europe and had costly "equipages" and many servants. Their reputation for hospitality, however, had suffered injury "particularly in the lower country; by the flood of dissipation and extravagance, which has of late been introduced into the state."[40] Finally, Fanfare's flight from the country at the end of the play exactly parellels the removal of wealthy planters to Charleston during the hot weather.[41] In the novel, Fanfare departs for France. In the play, however, Roger reports that the peer has "taken himself off to Lon'non. The country got to be too hot for him, ha, ha, ha."

William Ioor's *Independence* is significant not only as one of the first plays of the South and the first of South Carolina. It is also a very early example of agrarianism in American literature and an expression of a vital movement of its time, Jeffersonian Republicism. Ioor's main character is an idealized potrait, drawn, nevertheless, from American life. Charles Woodville does not depend on others for his necessities and comforts, nor must he seek support from creditors, nor does he look to another to determine what his own thinking and actions should be. He possesses to the fullest that quality most highly valued by Jefferson and his followers: independence.

Independence is a clear example of a play designed to influence political thinking, as is the next by Ioor. They are representative plays of this period since they express Republican ideas, which were growing stronger in South Carolina and the nation. These views, however, were strongly opposed in Charleston by the Federalists.

The Battle of Eutaw Springs

William Ioor's *Battle of Eutaw Springs* was the first play to dramatize a Revolutionary battle in the South. The war in the North had already received representation in such popular plays as John Daly Burk's *Bunker Hill* (1797), and William Dunlap's *The Glory of Columbia* (1803). Ioor selected the struggle that had inspired Philip Freneau in 1781 to write his stirring poem, "At Eutaw Springs the Valiant Died."

The Battle of Eutaw Springs is particularly important because it is an antecedent of the glorification of the Revolution that occurred in South Carolina from the 1820's to the Civil War. George C. Rogers, Jr. states that in the 1820's, because of economic decline (partly due to competition from Northern ports and the shift from commerce to industry) and attacks on slavery, Charleston turned to the historic past for reassurance. There was an idolization of Revolutionary heroes. This was the day of Parson Weems' *George Washington* and *Francis Marion,* but in South Carolina the key work was Alexander Garden's *Anecdotes of the Revolutionary War in America* (1822).[42] He idolized William Moultrie, William Washington, and Francis Marion, the same heroes acclaimed in Ioor's *Battle of Eutaw Springs.* The veneration in literary form that was done by Garden in 1822 was most notably continued by Simms, beginning with *The Partisan* in 1835. It had been done earlier by Ioor, however, in 1807.

The blend of spectacle, fiction and Southern history in *The Battle of Eutaw Springs* is noteworthy. The outdoor historical dramas of Paul Green which have spread through the South and the nation, are its modern descendants since they possess the same ingredients and appeal to the same interests.

Ioor's second play, like *Independence,* supports the Republican Party. It provides explicit evidence of Ioor's political sympathies. On the title page appears this statement: "Dedication. To the Republicans of South Carolina in general; but to those in particular who honored the theatre with their presence, on the two first nights of its representation."[43] Ioor's open declaration of party preference in 1807, possibly due to the increasing strength of the Republican Party in South Carolina, succeeded the indirect and covert expression of Jeffersonian Republicanism in his drama of 1805.

Produced during the period preceding the War of 1812, this play had a specific political purpose: to encourage a defiant stand and oppose a submissive attitude toward Great Britain. Ioor wished to revive the spirit that had previously motivated the new republic in its struggle with the mother country. In order to understand this purpose, it is essential to know the contemporary political situation.

When the Napoleonic Wars resumed in 1803, American neutrality faced new tests. After Great Britain changed to a stricter
policy regarding the shipment of cargo to French ports in 1805,
the seizure of American vessels increased sharply. On February 12,
1806, a Senate resolution attacked these actions and the impressment of American seamen (claimed to be British subjects) as a violation of neutral rights. Great Britain took no heed, and on April
18, 1806, Congress passed the Non-Importation Act, which, if put
into effect, would have prohibited importation of many items from
Great Britain. When James Monroe entered negotiations in London concerning Amreica's neutral rights on August 27, 1806, the
threat of stopping British imports was used. Though there was considerable debate as to the correct policy to follow, public opinion
against Great Britain increased, especially as a result of the impressment of American seamen.

The controversy over our relationship with Great Britain was evident in South Carolina. The Congressional delegation, which was
entirely Republican, supported the measures advocated by the Jefferson administration. The Federalists, on the other hand, favored a
more conciliatory policy. Their position was most cogently argued
in the "Phocian" letters starting in the Federalist *Courier* early in
1806. The author, the well-known Federalist William Loughton
Smith, said that greater demands based on neutrality were being
made of Great Britain than were warranted. He charged that the
only purpose of the Jefferson administration was "embroiling us
with England." In the election of 1806, the *Courier* asked that Smith
be sent to Congress, but he was defeated. The outcome of the election showed that South Carolina was still strongly Republican.[44]

In this atmosphere of political controversy, Ioor in 1806 composed his play depicting British defeat. The main plot covers the
American maneuvers immediately before the battle, the conflict itself, and the direct consequence: the retreat and evacuation of the
British from Charleston. The principal historical personages are

Generals Nathanael Greene and Francis Marion. Several others prominent in the fighting are characters, like Lieutenant Colonel William Washington. Lesser known figures also appear, such as Captain Laurence Manning, who became Adjutant General of South Carolina. Two subjects, designed to provide human interest, thrills, and humor, concern a young woman who becomes the bride of General Greene and a comic British soldier who decides to choose American citizenship at the end of the play.

Ioor's aim of advocating a bold stand against Great Britain in 1807 is seen in statements by characters and in the anti-British nature of many scenes. Three speakers stress the need for future generations to continue the endeavors begun during the Revolution. Ioor expresses through General Greene the notion of a possible Second War of Independence when the general says that our posterity will complete Washington's work if we do not. In the first scene, General Greene refers to the task of keeping the new nation "sacred and inviolable," and connects future Americans with a long roster of heroes: "Believe me, our posterity will, if we do not, complete the work which Warren, Washington, . . . the Pinckneys, and eke a thousand others have . . . so resolutely begun." Captain Laurence Manning, in the final scene, also links his own and succeeding generations. This officer hopes and prays that "the blessings of PEACE, INDEPENDENCE, PROSPERITY, and UNANIMITY, (*without which we never should have obtained our Independence*) may be handed down, pure and unsullied *to our latest posterity*; and enjoyed by them in the highest perfection, 'till after they all are dead." A third character also speaks of future generations. "The Genius of Liberty" appears in a vision to General Greene as he wonders to himself what the years ahead hold for his country. She promises that America will become a free, powerful, and virtuous nation and will so continue till the world's end, "*if her sons be but united and true to their interests*" (III.iii). Because of the division of Americans over relations with Great Britain, the references of the last two speakers to unity would carry special significance. All of the preceding statements emphasize the need for Americans of every generation to maintain the Spirit of '76, which in 1897 meant a defiance of Great Britain's hostile actions. These remarks make plain that Ioor did not believe America had achieved full independence.

The clearest evidence of Ioor's political purpose appears in the pervasive anti-British tone of the drama. Ioor made no secret of this aspect since he stated in a letter to the *City Gazette* published on July 16, 1806, that the object of the play was "to exalt the American character, and, possibly, depress that of the British government." The play presents the British as cruel opponents of American independence. In the first scene, General Greene, reviewing the causes of the war, says that a set of ministers "whose God is gold, and Bible, the ALCORAN!" decided to rule Americans with an iron rod. The image of the British as they leave Charleston is especially villainous. Hearing that the city is to be evacuated, the British soldiers say they will plunder and carry off enough spoil to keep them comfortable for the rest of their lives. One particularly detestable officer, Major Henry Barry, wishes that the war had been an "exterminating" one, "which we've for eight years waged, against *these bastard Britons*!" (V.i)

Another anti-British portion of the play appears in the subplot about a comic British soldier. Oliver Matthew Queerfish was recruited into service by force and dislikes fighting Americans since they are "our own dear countrymen" (I.ii). In the end he announces his intention to become an American citizen. The mere depiction of such a character and his remarks would add to the general anti-British animus, but it appears probable that Ioor is also alluding to the most burning issue between the United States and Great Britain at this time: the impressment of seamen from American vessels.

The experience of many British sailors and the story of Queerfish bear a number of similarities. During the wars of Napoleon, conditions on His Majesty's warships were so barbarous that the navy had to be recruited by press gangs. Men both on land and on merchant ships were seized in this way, and British subjects, especially sailors, sought sanctuary on American ships. Many secured naturalization papers and became American citizens. Great Britain, however, did not recognize naturalization of such subjects and impressed them when discovered on American ships.[45] In the play, Queerfish explains that he was recruited by force because he was mistaken for a sailor. After a successful performance at the circus in London, he invited his friends to "kick up a row" by dressing as sailors and attending the theater. On his way home a "press-gang" seized him "notwithstanding, I told them I was not the thing I seem'd; that I was no sailor, but Oliver Matthew Queerfish, esq. comedian" (I.ii). After the Battle of Eutaw Springs, Queerfish decides that he will "go to Genral, get a discharge—become an AMERICAN CITIZEN" (V.i). To a contemporary audience the decision of Queerfish would resemble sufficiently that of British sailors who became American citizens to gain its approval.

In addition to presenting a well-known military event, *The Battle of Eutaw Springs* provides an informative depiction of civil life during the Revolution. This aspect comes out most noticeably through the creation of fictional characters like Emily Bloomfield. Emily is the fiancée of General Greene and joins him at the end of the play. Ioor altered facts to suit his dramatic purposes here. Greene was already married before the Revolution to Catherine Littlefield, whose name is evidently the basis of "Bloomfield' in the play. She joined her husband in South Carolina on April 5, 1782, several months after the Battle of Eutaw Springs. Mrs. Greene's arrival was hailed as a symbol of peace coming to a devastated land. From this time on, she was the first lady of the South and after the liberation of Charleston a center of attraction in that city.[46]

Emily's part in the play brings to the forefront an important part of the Revolution: the civil strife between Tory and Whig, which was especially vicious in South Carolina.[47] At the time General Greene came to the state, the frenzy between Whigs and Tories was continuing unabated. He attempted to reestablish civil peace and gave orders for the protection of Whig and Tory families from outlaws of both parties.[48]

At the beginning of Act. IV, Emily enters with a Tory "plunderer," McGirt, in pursuit. In a highly melodramatic scene she begs Captain Manning to defend her. He does so by killing the villain in a duel. Before dying, McGirt confesses his misdeeds, among which is the admission that he dishonored respectable women "before the eyes of their manacled husbands."

Emily then describes the tragedy of her family. While the men of the family were at home on leave, McGirt and other "Tory plunderers" arrived and decided on "half hanging" her father to find out where their wealth was hidden. Her brother died opposing them, her mother was killed from a fall down the staircase, and the hanging of her father was completed. Finally, the plunderers set fire to "our elegant mansion," and while they tried "to inveigle away the negroes," she escaped.

In contrast to the dastardly Tory are members of an admirable Whig family, Jonathan Slyboots and his son. The curious name "Slyboots" is probably taken from a pro-Republican correspondent who used the name as a pseudonym in writing to the Republican *City Gazette* in 1805.[49] Jonathan exemplifies the best qualities of American patriots and South Carolinians. In the first scene of Act II, Queerfish seeks refuge in the Slyboots' cottage after being attacked by Whig plunderers while on sentry duty. Following a conversation which reveals his humorous nature, Old Slyboots offers Queerfish a meal and listens sympathetically to the hardships of the former actor's life. He says that every "child of sorrow" should be treated "by a native of the hospitable, and charitable state of South Carolina," as his brother.

Later in the play, Young Slyboots rejoices that he can deliver the news of the British evacuation to his father. He feels that this event will prolong the old man's life a score of years. The patriotism of his father is equal to that of Brutus, who did not love his country "with more enthusiastic, and more truly patriotic ardour, than does the humble yeoman who gave me birth' (V.i). The reference to "yeoman," that is, a small farmer who works his own land, is significant since it shows that in his second as well as his first play, Ioor portrayed the small independent farmer as a model American.

At the end of the play, Old Slyboots' protection of a lady in distress becomes known, but he indignantly refuses General Greene's reward for taking care of Emily Bloomfield. Slyboots says that the "Washington of Rhode-Island" does not know him or he would never have offered him "that which keeps the miser awake." He performed "a most important christian duty" by giving "succour to an unprotetced, helpless female!" Slyboots wins the honor of giving Emily away in marriage and is dubbed "Old Hospitality" by Laurence Manning.

Jonathan Slyboots stands out in Ioor's play as his most distinctive fictional creation. Recembling such country gentlemen as Frank Meriwether of John Pendleton Kennedy's *Swallow Barn* and Simms's Captain Porgy, he possesses the characteristics that have come to be associated with that type in Southern literature: hospitality, a penchant for rhetorical flourishes in speaking, a chivalric concern for women, and a humorous tone balancing the serious. The early date of this composition makes him a prototypical figure.[30]

It is interesting to compare *The Battle of Eutaw Springs* with Simms's Revolutionary romances about the same events. The play includes many of the same elements found in the romances: British avarice, the Whig-Tory conflict, cruel Tory plunderers, and the combination of historical and fictional persons. Both Ioor and Simms presented the Scots in South Carolina as loyalists. Ioor named a Tory plunderer "McGirt." Simms stated that the Scots were resolutely loyalist, in contrast to the Scotch-Irish, who were Whigs (*The Forayers*, Chapter 1). He named the Tory villain in *Woodcraft* M'Kewn. Simms owned a copy of Ioor's play and wrote that in South Carolina it was "among the first if not the very first, native dramas brought on the boards."[51] A noteworthy similarity in the play and in Simms's *Eutaw* is the phenomenon of visions. In the drama, General Greene sees the Genius of Liberty, who tells him of America's future (II.iii). Throughout the novel, the clairvoyant Hurricane Nell has visions of the fate of characters, such as the hanging of her lawless brother.[52]

Since Ioor announced in his letter to the *City Gazette* (July 16, 1806) that he purposed "telling a plain, unvarnished tale of truth" about a historical event, it is appropriate to make a comparison with other accounts, both early and more recent. Judgment of Ioor's presentation of the battle was already being made by his contemporaries. After seeing the play, a correspondent to the *City Gazette* (January 14, 1807) stated that *The Battle of Eutaw Springs* was "a faithful record" of the event.

Published descriptions of the battle were available for Ioor to read. In a "Note" on works consulted for his *Life of Francis Marion*, Simms listed, among others printed before 1806, *The History of the Revolution of South-Carolina from a British Province to an Independent State* (1785), by the respected historian David Ramsay and *Memoirs of the American Revolution* (1802), by General William Moultrie.[53] Facts and descriptions in these two works indicate that Ioor drew on them for his play. For example, the figures for American and British losses in the battle are exactly the same in all three works. Furthermore, Ioor prints verbatim a letter sent to Moultrie that is included in the general's *Memoirs*.[54]

The play agrees with subsequent histories as to the general nature of the event. It presents the battle as the final step toward expelling the British and as an outstanding demonstration of American bravery. John Chester Miller calls Eutaw Springs "the last important battle to be fought in the South during the Revolutionary War." Another historian, Theodore Thayer, notes that both sides claimed a victory, but if Eutaw Springs was a victory for the British, "it was of the kind that led to certain ruin." He remarks that perhaps in no general contest in the whole war did the American militia fight so valiantly and successfully.[55]

In regard to specific details of the battle, there are both similarities and interesting differences between the play and other versions.[56] In the second scene of Act II, a "rooting party" of British soldiers, sent out to dig sweet potatoes, first sees the advancing Americans, and Queerfish carries back the alarm to the British commander, Colonel Stewart. Captain Manning says that if it had not been for the rooting party, the Americans would have "completely surprised the enemy's main body." A statement about this episode in Moultrie's *Memoirs,* similar even in langauge, evidences further that Ioor knew this work. Moultrie writes that it was unfortunate that this British party was encountered; "otherwise their main body would have been completely surprised."[57]

Later writers describe this prelude to the battle differently. They say that while the rooting party was gone, two American deserters informed Colonel Stewart of the imminent attack. Although the commander was inclined not to believe them, he sent out Major John Coffin with a detachament to reconnoiter. When Coffin met the Americans, a few of his horsemen galloped back to camp and gave the warning.[58]

A brave American officer, Lieutenant Colonel William Washington, figures prominently in the play. The episode of Washington's horse being shot out from under him and the sparing of his life is repeated in several histories.[59] Ioor adds a memorable detail not found in the histories: Just as Washington is about to be killed, he gives a Masonic sign. This is recognized by a British officer, who is a fellow Mason. He commands that Washington's life be spared and exclaims: "Oh, that we were but friends! accursed war!" (III.iv)

Statistics on battle casualties vary considerably. Ioor's figures are more favorable to the American side than those cited by modern historians. According to Greene and Marion in the play, the Americans took 600 prisoners. The British lost over 1100 in killed and wounded; the Americans, not up to 500 (IV.ii). Neither Edward McCrady, David Duncan Wallace, nor Theodore Thayer set the British losses as high as Ioor; Thayer's statistics are closest to those in the play. He states that the Americans took over 400 prisoners and lost 500 men. The number of British losses "could very well have been 900," but he believes the estimate of 1000 is too high.[60]

The colorful march into Charleston at the close of the play is also described in other works. Simms wrote that the balconies were "crowded with joyous faces." The best-selling author Parson Mason Weems, writing with General Peter Horry, recounted that the ladies of the city flew to their windows and balconies, waving handkerchiefs that "but half concealed their angel blushes."[61]

The most noticeable difference between Ioor's battle scene and subsequent accounts is the absence in the play of the disorderly pilfering of the enemy camp by the thirsty American soldiers. The dramatist's account, however, agrees with Ramsay's and Moultrie's reports, which do not mention this failure of American discipline in the midst of the contest. Later historians invariably include it. Simms is very critical. In *Eutaw,* he states that the soldiers, "fastening upon the liquors," became unmanageable. Captain Porgy, a militiaman with Francis Marion's Partisans, blames the Continentals, saying the battle was lost "by the dispersion of our regulars among the tents; by the mad fury with which they fastened upon rum and brandy." McCrady also refers to the drinking of the Americans in the tents, which caused them to become unmanageable. According to Robert D. Bass, the fleeing British line was saved by the pilfering; the American officers lost control, and Greene ordered a retreat. Thayer also refers to this disorganization in the hour of triumph, but declines to call it the sole cause of an incomplete victory.[62]

The foregoing comparison of the play with other accounts of the battle reveals that the dramatist furnished some special touches of his own. For instance, Ioor includes such colorful details as the dialogue between Lieutenant Colonel Washington and the British officer on discovering they are fellow Masons. Since Ioor grew up in the years following the Revolution and lived close to the battle site, he must have heard tales drawn from the memories of soldiers and other persons as did Simms. The Revolution was a principal inspiration for future authors growing up in South Carolina during its aftermath, as can be seen also in reports on the childhood of John Blake White and William Gilmore Simms.[63]

Newspaper Comment on
The Battle of Eutaw Springs

Contemporary reaction to *The Battle of Eutaw Springs* is preserved in the two rival newspapers of Charleston: the Federalist *Courier* and the Republican *City Gazette*. Half a year before the first production of the play, a journalistic debate occurred. Later, after the production in January, 1807, the *Gazette* published laudatory comments, but the *Courier* took no notice of the play.

The first newspaper consideration of *The Battle of Eutaw Springs* took place in July, 1806. On July 2, Ioor printed a letter in the *City Gazette* under the pseudonym of "W. J. Youngschool" concerning proposals for printing his play. He gave a brief description of the work and a short extract in verse.[64] This letter was directed at potential subscribers to his play.

Six days later in the *Courier,* July 8, 1806, a comment appeared finding fault with the play as described by Ioor. The writer stated that it was "indelicate to introduce living characters into a play." The incidents to be dramatized were so recent that the audience would be "very naturally engaged in separating the fictitious from the true part of the story. Distraction will of course ensue, interest is out of the question." Furthermore, this critic found that the verse did not *"chime"*: It was verse run "ideot" [sic]. Since the dramatist chose the name "Youngschool," he would show his rejection of such innovations by taking the name of "Oldschool."

This letter drew from Ioor a long, spirited rebuttal in the *City Gazette* of July 16, 1806. He stated that after the proposals for printing were issued, there were many people who believed no such play was ready to be published. Accordingly he sent a letter to the *Gazette* confirming its existence and included a summary and extracts from memory. "Oldschool" should have waited to see the whole text before attacking it, only one-fourth of which was in blank verse.

Ioor undertook to answer specific charges made by his critic. In regard to portraying living characters, he cited the precedent of Washington in William Dunlap's "popular play of 'The Glory of Columbia—Her Yeomanry!'" It was acted repeatedly before the general's death. As for the attack on his verse, Ioor replied, "If the lines in the extracts alluded to are not poetical; they are at least patriotic ones." The objection to the verse, however, was eventually accepted; the printed play is entirely in prose except for verse quotations from other authors.

"Oldschool" in his letter had concluded from the *dramatis personae* that the author intended to introduce "ludicrous circumstances" rather than give dignity to the performance. Ioor defended the inclusion of a "mirth-creating character" since "every playwright must, of necessity, have an eye to the stage-effect of his piece."[65] He cited Shakespeare's use of Falstaff in the two parts of *King Henry IV* and sarcastically observed that even "Oldschool" would not say the great dramatist's purpose was to provide dignity in those cases.

Ioor aimed the sharpest language in his letter directly at his critic, who he assumed to be Stephen Cullen Carpenter, the editor and drama critic of the *Courier*. He declared that his opponent's purpose was in fact to prevent publication of the play. The American people, however, would thwart and would not let the opinion "of a foreigner carry any weight." He stated that since his play was an original American production, it would not fail to earn the denunciation of a *"self-created Censor Morum,* whose predilection for every thing monarchical, every thing aristocratical has been notorious ever since he took up his residence amongst us."

Ioor attempted to defend himself against further critical attacks when he published *The Battle of Eutaw Springs* in 1807. Verses quoted on the title page include these lines from Pope's *Essay on Criticism*:

> In Poets, as true genius is but rare,
> True taste as seldom is the Critic's share.
>
> (Part I, lines 11-12)

It is clear that Ioor believed his critic to be S. C. Carpenter though he does not state Carpenters' name. In his letter to the *Gazette* Ioor said that his critic had conversed with goblins in Ireland and was the son of a Dublin box-office keeper. Carpenter was in fact born in Ireland. In the *Courier,* July 19, 1806, Carpenter said he was not the person who had written the attacks in the *Courier* signed "Oldschool" as Ioor had accused him of doing.

The response in the *Courier* to Ioor's letter of July 16 was immediate and indignant. On July 17, 1806, the editors stated that S. C. Carpenter had never seen the letter of "Oldschool" until it appeared in the newspaper. The next day "Oldschool" wrote that he had criticized the merit, not the motives of the play. "Youngschool" should have printed the corrected verses of his extract; then he could have revised or confirmed his opinion. He also rebuked "Youngschool" for his remarks against Carpenter.

On July 19, 1806, a cutting reply to "Youngschool" appeared in the *Courier* with the name "S. C. Carpenter" at the end. Carpenter stated that he had never seen the first letter from "Oldschool" before its publication. Answering the personal references made about himself, he said that he was not the son of "a Dublin box-office keeper." He dismissed the other insinuations, saying that they had been bandied about "a thousand times." As for the composition, he asserted that a play must have more to redeem it than patriotism. Referring to the author, he said, "If he had nothing but his pen to live upon, he would be as poor as his own soldiers of Eutaw."

In the *Courier* of July 22, 1806, John Blake White took note of the controversy over *The Battle of Eutaw Springs*. He said that the play and certain pieces written in support of it had been ascribed to him. He then stated "unequivocally" that he had "no knowledge whatever of the play or its author."

The relationship of Ioor and Carpenter had known happier days as seen in the critic's prologue and highly complimentary review of Ioor's first play.[66] Now Carpenter speaks slightingly of Ioor and his writings. He believes that the author's "natural temper may have been a little soured by the reception of some of his works."

The argument between Ioor and Carpenter is interesting because it deals with a basic question. Does the aim of preserving the events of a people compensate for the lack of merit in writing? Simms and Arthur Hobson Quinn second Carpenter's evaluation that the play has faults. Simms wrote that the success of Ioor's play was "due rather to its patriotism than to his literary execution."[67] Quinn called the work "a chronical play of patriotic text rather than dramatic effectiveness."[69] These judgments are, however, too severe. Although *The Battle of Eutaw Springs* shows little distinction in language, and plotting, the diction is clear and varied according to the speaker, and the alternation of historical and fictional persons is well balanced. In any case, the paucity of dramatic compositions at this time assures an affirmative answer to the above question. The events and life of the new republic cried out for treatment in literary form, but few responded. It is now well accepted by scholars that early American plays possess a historical value not dependent on their literary merit.[69]

The positions taken toward *The Battle of Eutaw Springs* in the rival newspapers continued very noticeably after the first performance on January 10, 1807. It is impossible not to see a sign of the Federalist-Republican controversy in the complete ignoring of the play by the *Courier*. This organ of the Federalists printed no review nor letter, though in the same month it had run several communications about the non-political play of another native South Carolinian, *The Mysteries of the Castle,* by John Blake White.

The Republican *City Gazette,* on the other hand, published two long "Communications" dealing with Ioor's drama on January 14, 1807. "Aristophanes" stressed the patriotic quality. The purpose of the play was laudable, he said: "to render us familiar with the history of the period it celebrates, and to rescue from oblivion an event, which must ever be dear to Americans and Carolinians in particular." The characters were mostly drawn from real life, he noted, and would be interesting to those who have a fond remembrance of them.

The second "Communication" was submitted by "A Republican and Whig of '76."[70] This writer, first, expressed his pride in seeing such a number of "republicans" at the play by "our countryman, Dr. Ioor." He, then, made a strong appeal for support of the state's literature.

> But something of consequence to the *literary character* of this state of South-Carolina, yet remains to be done. Should we be found backward in encouraging the attempts at dramatic composition, by *our native citizens,* we may look forward in vain for the time when authors of celebrity will be the growth of the state which gave us birth. We have already made a handsome commencement; already can be boast of *a tragic* and *a comic* muse;[71] both of whom are entitled to the highest praise, due allowance being made for their youth and inexperience, as well as their want of those advantages which the authors of old countries have been, for centuries, in possession of.

In conclusion, this "Republican" called for support from the Society of Cincinnati[72] and the Whigs of '76. They should not allow it to be said that the author "of a correct history of the Battle of Eutaw Springs" lacked their support. It is clear that for the two supporters of Ioor's play, party loyalty and the desire to encourage a native literature prevailed over questions of literary quality.

IV

JOHN BLAKE WHITE

*B*ohn Blake White (1781-1859) was the first writer in the South to compose a substantial number of plays, five in all, three of which were performed. Because of this number and the long period over which his compositions appeared (1806 to 1837, covering the managements of Placide and Gilfert), he deserves recognition as the pioneer dramatist in the South, as William Dunlap does in the North. This honor was considered his due by *The National Cyclopaedia of American Biography,* which called him "the pioneer of literature and art in the South."[1] The most significant aspect of White's plays to modern readers is the shift from foreign plots to a concern with American life. From his first two plays, which have European settings and no relationship to contemporary American issues, White changed to works treating dueling, intemperance, and Andrew Jackson's Seminole War. He also left a notable achievement in painting, especially in historical works on American subjects. He reveals the aim of glorifying the Revolution through his paintings.

White was born on September 2, 1781, six days before the Battle of Eutaw Springs, the fourth child of Blake Leay and Elizabeth

BUST OF JOHN BLAKE WHITE IN THE CHARLESTON CITY HALL.
COURTESY, CITY OF CHARLESTON.
PHOTOGRAPH BY LARRY R. KENNEDY.

Bourquin White, at Whitehall Plantation, St. John's Parish, Berkeley County, South Carolina.[2] His birthplace was near the battleground itself. This battle and other Revolutionary scenes were to form a large part of his contribution to early American painting. White's family was prominent in the Revolution. His father fought at Ft. Moultrie and White showed him manning a gun in his painting *Defense of Ft. Moultrie,* now in the national Capitol.[3] His mother served as "a spy or visitor into the British Army in Charleston to furnish information to Marion in his fastnesses on the Pee Dee and Santee." During the first nine years of his life, which were spent at Whitehall, White often heard tales of the Revolution from visitors to his father's tavern.[4] Economic distress due to the Revolution forced White's father to move to Charleston, where he taught architecture and built houses. He died in 1796 from a fall while constructing a house.[5]

In 1800 White made plans to study painting under the famous American-born artist Benjamin West in England. He sailed for England on the *Amity,* which was captured by a French corvett, but rescued by two English frigates. Landing at Cork, Ireland, White attended the theatre there. He must have made a comparison with Charleston when he wrote that the theatre in Cork was "nothing superior to what I had been accustomed." In 1802 White recorded his presence at Sheridan's *Pizarro* in London and noted that he went frequently to the theatre, "the most lasting source of real enjoyment to me." He also attended the theatre in Oxford and Birmingham; in the latter city he saw a play by M. G. Lewis, the popular author of Gothic tales.[6]

In London White went to West's studio two or three times a week for two years. He adopted his teacher's view of painting, which stressed its moral essence. According to West, painting should assist the reason to receive moral influence by showing the effects of motives and passions.[7] This viewpoint influenced all of White's subsequent painting. Among White's friends in London, one was to attain high distinction. In 1801, he met Washington

Allston, a fellow South Carolinian who also studied with West. Allston wrote Charles Fraser, who became a successful miniaturist in Charleston: "Your friend White I like very much. He has a spice of literature about him which makes him not the less agreeable to me." White's lifelong fascination with the romantic and the Gothic, in which he reflects the insatiable taste of his age for the strange, began to take shape in England. In 1802 on a trip to the north of England, he described with great relish the "ruined Monasteries, Castles, and Abbays." At Bridgenorth on the Severn, he noted the forbidding aspect of the castle, which could have been the scene of one of the currently popular Gothic melodramas. White wrote: "The ruins of the Castle here are very fine. They are situated on an eminence, and lean in such a threatening situation as to strike terror and awe into the beholder."[8]

In November, 1803, White returned to Charleston from England. The *City Gazette,* December 6, advertised his availability for portrait painting. On June 5, 1804, he resolved to leave for Boston since he "found no encouragement for historical painting, that branch of the arts always the object of my ambition and delight." On August 30, 1894, he noted that he had discussed the prospects of painting in the United States with Timothy Ford, a South Carolina lawyer then in New England. White confided to him "how disappointed I was in not meeting with better success as I now knew by experience, that nothing but portrait painting could at present meet with sufficient encouragement in America." Ford offered him the chance to study law at his office, suggesting he would find "a certain resource in the Law."[9] White returned to South Carolina, and on March 28, 1805, married Elizabeth Allston, daughter of Francis Allston of Waccamaw. He had met this relative of Washington Allston while she was visiting in New England. Their first son, Edward Brickell White (1806-1882), became an outstanding architect.[10]

White entered the law office of Desaussure and Ford in Charleston on December 14, 1804, ten days before John C. Calhoun. The latter paid the fee of one hundred guineas, but by White's name in the "Cash Book" is the notation "not to pay fee." In 1806, while studying law, White wrote that he had some spare time which he employed "to advantage and I compleated a Tragedy which I had had in view some years before."[11]

White's first play, *Foscari,* a romantic tragedy in blank verse, was given at the Charleston Theatre on January 10, 13, and February 24, 1806, and on January 20, 1809.[12] It tells the story of Foscari, the son of the Doge of Venice. He has been falsely accused of murdering Count Donato, the father of Almeria, his beloved. After five years in Candia, Foscari returns and is tried again. He is permitted to leave prison temporarily and visits Almeria, who still believes him guilty. The real culprits, Erizzo and Policarpo, fail in their attempt to kill Foscari. Erizzo confesses his guilt, but the news arrives too late. Foscari has died of heartbreak. Almeria, in a scene at the end recalling Ophelia's derangement, goes mad, crying, "Despair, despair, distraction and the grave." This play contains most of the common elements of romantic plays. The Gothic influence appears in the attacks by the villains and in the gloomy prison scene, in which Foscari concludes sadly that Almeria has "forgot this heart still beats" (III.i). The villainous characters are presented as wholly evil with little effort to account for their motives.

Two manuscripts of this play are held by the South Carolina Historical Society, dated 1805 and 1806. In the first, at the end of Act. IV, White drew an ink sketch of Almeria fleeing from Policarpo and Erizzo. In the *Courier,* February 28, 1806, White thanked those who had subscribed to the publication of *Foscari.* They could obtain their copy "by applying at Mr. Hoff's Bookstore, Broad Street."

White's next play, *The Mysteries of the Castle,* was performed at the Charleston Theatre on December 26, 29, 1806 and February 19, 1807. The "Friend" who wrote the prologue says that this play embraces a wider range than the preceding since it contains

"A Cast'le, Myst'ry, Victim and Revenge."[13] Oral Coad writes that in this play "ghosts, explosions, and underground passages provide enough adventures for half a dozen melodramas."[14] In this revenge melodrama, Fauresco, the villain, once loved Elienora, who became the wife of the Count de Mainfrois. He killed Elenora's brother, but made it appear that de Mainfrois had done the deed. De Mainfrois is forced to live as a hermit until finally reunited with his wife and daughter in the subterranean chambers of his castle. Fauresco tries to finish his revenge on de Mainfrois by blowing up the castle, but only buries himself in the explosion. The final catastrophe points up White's moral clearly enough, but the actor who played Fauresco reiterates it in the epilogue. He admonishes the audience to learn the results of jealousy and revenge from this play. The element of Gothic horror appears particularly in a spectre of the castle, who turns out to be a robber.

The villain's demonic aims make him the most forceful and interesting character. Fauresco, who admits, "My idol, is Revenge!" (IV.v), provoked a spirited argument in the *Courier* (January 3 and 7, 1807). A correspondent named "Stefanolf" attacked the characterization and was refuted by "Philo-Fauresco." Two attitudes toward the Gothic in drama appear in their positions. According to Stefanolf, violent emotions may effect "an excellent moral lesson," but not when the mind cannot understand their cause. He cannot discover why Fauresco calls himself the "evil genius" of de Mainfrois. He objects to a character abnormally different from other human beings since human nature is ever the same. "Philo-Fauresco" answers that he cannot allow Stefanolf's knowledge of human nature "to be commensurate with his critical skill." Anyone acquainted with the secret workings of the human heart should be able to account for the hatred of such a character as Fauresco toward the man whom he had injured once before. The innocence shown by Stefanolf does more credit to the heart of a man than to the pen of the critic. The popularity of this play in Charleston is indicated by an announcement in the *Courier*,

February 3, 1807: "The Thistle Club" proudly subscribed for one hundred copies.

White wrote three more plays. *Modern Honor* was presented at the Charleston Theatre in 1812. The *Triumph of Liberty* was published on May 3, 1819, but not performed. His last play, *The Forgers,* was published in five issues of the *Southern Literary Journal* in 1837.[15] These three plays are his most important dramatic writings since they show his shift to American life and problems; they will be examined at length below.

With admittance to the bar in January 5, 1808, White's financial prospects improved. In the years ahead he participated prominently in the civic and cultural activities of the city and achieved a high standing in the community. On March 4, 1811, he delivered an "Oration on the Federal Constitution" to the patriotic '76 Association.[16] During the War of 1812 he was commissioned a Deputy Quartermaster General of the Militia of South Carolina on August 15, 1812.[17] In 1813 the Literary and Philosophical Society was formed in Charleston, and White soon became an active member. He read several essays there and donated $750 to its library fund.[18] This society with its cultural and educational aims was comparable to the lyceum in New England and lasted until 1860. Meetings were held at the homes of members every two weeks between October and May. Presidents included such well-known citizens as Thomas Grimké, Timothy Ford, and Joel R. Poinsett. Hugh Swinton Legaré read "On the Greek Republic" before this group. From about 1825 to 1860 there were few notable visitors in the South whom it did not entertain.[19]

In 1812 White openly avowed the Democratic-Republican cause by standing for the state legislature on that ticket. He lost in this race as he did for Secretary of State in 1814, and for the legislature again in 1816. In 1818, however, he was elected state representative from the district of St. Philip's and St. Michael's. During his term he served on the committee to study the establishment of a lunatic asylum in Charleston.[20] Prestige as a legislator led to more

legal practice and partnership with F. A. Deliesseline in the firm of
White and Deliesseline.[21] As a leading citizen he took part in the
welcome of President James Monroe in 1819.[22] White next supported the South Carolina Academy of Fine Arts, which received
its charter in 1821 and became the most important cultural organization of the decade in the city. On February 17, 1821, the
Courier announced that Joel R. Poinsett would be the first president and White a director.

In 1817 White's wife died. He wrote movingly of this loss in
his journal and described the consolation received from a favorite
book of his wife's, "The New Manual of Devotion." On October 1,
1819, he was married to Ann Rachel O'Driscoll, daughter of Dr.
Matthew O'Driscoll of Charleston.[23]

In 1826, White joined his brother James J. B. White in running
a paper factory. Located at Bull Sluice, Lexington District, it was
the only paper mill in South Carolina for some ten years.[24] For
five years he was connected with this venture and lived at Tuscu-
lum, about ten miles above Columbia. The enterprise ended when
the mill was destroyed by fire at a loss of $20,000.[25] When White
returned to Charleston in 1832, the Nullification controversy was
raging and he allied himself with the Unionists. He had previously
made known his support of the federal government in such ways
as his oration on the Constitution and his long assocation with
Joel R. Poinsett and Thomas Smith Grimké, leaders of the Union
Party. The former had been his friend since his trip to Boston in
1804, and admiration for the latter caused him to name a son
Thomas Grimké White.[26]

At this period of his life, White gave increasing attention to
painting, which must fill a large place in any account of his activities. Though White abandoned a career as an artist, he continued to devote much of his time not spent on law to painting.
Simms praised his design and grouping but not his "finish."[27]
White's paintings reveal the influence of drama. Paul Partridge
points out that a primary characteristic of all White's historical and

romantic paintings is "the fact that he approached the subject matter as a dramatist, carefully selecting the most dramatic moment of the event, and grouping his figures to achieve the highest degree of dramatic intensity." He states that this characeristic is well indicated in White's painting *The Battle of New Orleans*,[28] which was done in 1817, two years before he published a play on the same subject, *The Triumph of Liberty*. Paintings which show the romantic features of his first two plays are *The Grave Robbers* (1833)[29] and *Conrad and Gulnare from Byron's "Corsair"* (1835).

The interrelationship of painting and literature in White's mind appears in a lecture delivered on March 9, 1832, to the Literary and Philosophical Society: "An Essay on the Moral Excellence of Painting and shewing the superiority of its powers over those of Poetry."[30] White, first, describes the ideal, a merging of painting and poetry. In painting, he says, everything depends on the poetical conception of the subject since "the painter must catch the same fire and spirit that glows within the bosom of the Poet, or else his productions must be devoid of interest." Painting is superior to poetry, he states, because it does not depend on a changing medium like language that separates the modern reader from "the poetry of Chaucer, Spenser, or Burns." As for "the moral excellence" of painting, which his teacher Benjamin West had stressed, White lists these effects: "It enlarges the mind, purifies the heart, chastens, polishes the taste, corrects and improves the understanding."

After entering the legal profession in 1802, White did a charming portrait of his family, including himself, but little other painting until 1816.[31] On August 5, 1816, the *Courier* described his *Battle of New Orleans,* which was exhibited in 1825 before Lafayette on his visit to Charleston.[32] White offered this painting and his *Battle of Eutaw Springs* (1825) to the state. The House of Representatives thanked him for his "liberal offer" and the canvases were hung in the Senate Chamber. Both were destroyed in the burning of Columbia, February 17, 1865.[33] On February 21, 1827, the *Courier* announced the exhibition of *The Defense of Fort Moultrie;* it now hangs in the Senate Gallery, South Corridor, the national Capitol. This painting shows one of White's most successful uses of color; blues, reds, and browns stand out vividly.[34]

White's most productive period as a painter was from 1834 to 1839. The achievements of these years show that in the career of this amateur artist there was a progressive movement toward better work. In 1834, White finished a painting that brought him national recognition, *The Unfurling of the United States Flag at Mexico* (also called *The Flag*). Widely exhibited, it occasioned comment in New Orleans, Washington, Philadelphia, and New York. It depicted the following scene during a revolution in Mexico City on November 30, 1828. After the European Spaniards pursued by "the native Mexicans" had taken refuge at the American Embassy, Joel R. Poinsett, the ambassador, came to the balcony and unfurled the American flag; he "demanded that all persons in his house should be protected while the flag of his country waved over them." The scene of confusion changed and the attackers cheered the banner.[35] In this painting, as in his play *The Triumph of Liberty,* White championed a current political position. The anti-Nullification implications of *The Flag* were recognized from the first. The *Courier,* December 10, 1834, was glad that it attracted "visitors of both parties," though it recognized the Unionists as "the originators of the work." The central character in the scene was Poinsett, leader of the Union Party in Charleston, and the painting enforced the principal argument of this group; the national government must not allow its power to be set aside by any of the states. In a letter to the American painter John Trumbull in July, 1835, White wrote that a committee requested this painting from him and named its members. They were the leaders of the Union Party in South Carolina.[36] This canvas was declined by the United States Senate, but accepted by Andrew Jackson, who bequeathed it to the Carolinian who would display the most valor

*General Marion in His Swamp Encampment Inviting
a British Officer to Dinner* (or *The Camp of Marion*),
ENGRAVING AFTER THE PAINTING BY JOHN BLAKE WHITE.
COURTESY, ANNE S. K. BROWN MILITARY COLLECTION,
BROWN UNIVERSITY LIBRARY.

in defense of his country. In 1858, it was given to the "Palmetto Regiment" for service in the Mexican War.[37] It was destroyed in the burning of Columbia.

The favorable reception of *The Flag* provided an impetus to White's painting. In September, 1836, he completed *General Marion in His Swamp Encampment Inviting a British Officer to Dinner*. Variously called *The Camp of Marion* or *The Potato Dinner*, it is probably his best-known work. By copy and reproduction through engraving it reached more Americans than *The Flag*. White made at least four versions, one of which now hangs in the Capitol. Another of the versions and an engraving may be seen at the South Caroliniana Library. The painting was engraved by Sartain of Philadelphia for the Apollo Association in 1841, and an engraving was used on the five dollar bank notes of South Carolina in 1861 and 1872.[38] This painting is approximately twenty-eight by thirty-six inches and shows the camp of Marion bordering the Santee during the time of his guerilla warfare against the British occupation of Charleston, 1782–83. The British officer visits under a flag of truce to discuss exchange of prisoners and is invited by the "Swamp Fox" to a meal of sweet potatoes. According to Partridge, the primitive life of the patriots is realistically depicted by crude shelters, makeshift clothing and equipment, and their meager fare. By contrast, the figures of Marion and the British officer are highly romanticized. Both wear spotlessly clean knee trousers and brass-buttoned uniforms. The Briton is more stylishly clad, but Marion is not shown of inferior grade in rank or dress. The only homely note is the fur hat and powder horn slung at Marion's waste. The other figures are in motley and varied dress and equipment. The dark complexioned frontiersmen with their feathered caps and mustaches are reminiscent of characters in contemporary melodramas. The Negro servant especially is drawn realistically. The trees hung with Spanish moss plus the naturalness of the high banks of the river indicate a knowledge of the area. White manages to give some sense of the dampness and silence of the retreat.

Partridge calls this painting "not a very successful attempt at depicting an historical incident." The face of Marion "gives little indication of the traditional dauntless character of the man." The main interest of the observer today lies in "its anecdotal elements" (that is, realistic treatments of contemporary subject matter), and those are almost entirely confined to the left half of the canvas, where the Negro is cooking sweet potatoes.[39] For the student of literature, nevertheless, the blend of romanticism and realism is noteworthy since this is seen also in Ioor's *Battle of Eutaw Springs* and all of Simms's Revolutionary romances. Further, *The Camp of Marion* epitomizes the glorification of the Revolution in South Carolina, which received an impetus in the 1820's from Major Alexander Garden's *Anecdotes of the Revolutionary War* and continued during the years when Simms's works appeared.

In 1837, White completed his *Arrival of the Mail* (also called *Perspective View of Broad Street*), the best of his anecdotal paintings. It is now in the Council Chamber, Charleston City Hall. In 1837, White exhibited the fourth work in his series about the Revolution: *Sergeant Jasper Rescuing American Prisoners from the British Soldiers near Savannah, Georgia* (also called *The Rescue*). In 1838, he completed *The Conflagration of St. Philip's Church* (now in the vestibule of that church, Charleston). Anna Wells Rutledge calls this highly emotional scene of people running about and grieving one of White's most interesting paintings from today's point of view.[40] The following year White finished another Revolutionary scene: *Mrs. Motte Inviting General Marion and Colonel Lee to Burn Her Residence* (also called *The Burning Arrows*). Now in the Capitol, it depicts Mrs. Motte handing a bundle of arrows to the general.

From 1841 to 1850, White was involved in projects for the engraving of *The Rescue* and *The Flag*. In a letter dated June 21, 1841, White requested Judge R. M. Charlton of Savannah to subscribe to the engravings of *The Rescue*.[41] The subscription campaign for *The Rescue* was successful, but *The Flag* was never done by an engraver.[42] White completed his Revolutionary series in 1850 with *The Martyrdom of Hayne* and *The Capture of André*.[43]

For his accomplishments in painting, White was elected to honorary membership in the National Academy of Design, the *Courier* announced on July 23, 1845. Its president was the famous artist Samuel F. B. Morse. The following facts stand out in a summary of White's achievements as a painter. First, four works have been honored by being hung in the Capitol: *The Defense of Ft. Moultrie, The Camp of Marion, The Burning Arrows,* and *The Rescue.* Second, White completed an impressive array of Revolutionary paintings: those just named plus *The Battle of Eutaw Springs, The Martyrdom of Hayne* and *The Capture of André.* Third, he did portraits of the leading South Carolinians of his age, such as Charles Cotesworth Pinckney, Governor Henry Middleton, John C. Calhoun, and Francis Marion.[44]

In 1848 White's position as a leading writer and painter in Charleston was recognized by the anonymous author of *The Vindication,* a booklet in answer to *Charleston, A Satire,* which deprecated the literature of the city.[45] White's name appears first in a list of Charleston writers:

First in the Band, lo! noble White is seen,
The youthful Dramatist of seventeen: [46]
Whose Plays, the offspring of a generous mind,
Must warm all hearts to VIRTUE'S paths inclined.
Once more within "THE CASTLE"[47] now I roam
A wanderer, raptured with th' enchanted home:
Once more I weep at poor "FOSCARI'S" side,
And curse the wretches who the wrack applied!
Here "MODERN HONOR" hath too sadly taught
What hellish deeds by *Honor* oft are wrought!
"THE FORGERS" next the awful truth teach well:—
Vice is the path which leads thee on to HELL!
These in his left—his right-hand in, behold.
The Bard inspiring all the Artist's soul:—

Here MARION, MOULTRIE, SUMPTER, LEE, command[48]
Once more, in canvas, 'neath his Magic-Wand.
And, while I gaze, hark, e'en from England's shore,
His well-earned praises proudly wafted o'er![49]

During the years of his best painting after returning to Charleston in 1832, White filled a position at the Custom House, having given up the practice of law. On March 10, 1837, he appealed to his old friend Poinsett for a better position, stating that the job was not adequate for his expenditures "nor conformable to my taste and habits."[50] Nothing seems to have come of this request since he remained in the position till 1857 when a codicil to his will states that he relinquished the work because of physical inability.[51] His residence at this time, according to his will, was 21 Legaré Street. In 1839 White was selected by the City Council as Clerk and Treasurer of the Board of Supervisors of the High School of Charleston, a position he held until his death.[52] At the end of his life White's children provided him an annuity of $500.[53]

When White died on August 24, 1859, the *Courier* took note of his achievements and stated that those of the past generation who worked in "social, moral, intellectual, and aesthetic efforts" found in him "a zealous assistant."[54] Partridge makes a judicious estimate of his special place in American culture. He should be remembered "not only as a man who represents in his own life a synthesis of the cultural and intellectual forces of ante-bellum Charleston, but also as a pioneer romantic in the South of 1800-1860, and as an artist who successfully achieved a fusion of the two art forms of drama and painting."[55]

Reform Plays:
Modern Honor and *The Forgers*

As a dramatist, White is most distinctive as an early writer of reform plays. *Modern Honor* is the first anti-dueling play in America and *The Forgers* is one of the first temperance dramas. As will be seen, these plays were part of White's long dedication to social reform. Although the reform movement never attained the success in the South that it did in the North, it created great fervor among certain Southerners. Such a man was Thomas S. Grimké, a close friend of White's in Charleston, who vigorously supported reforms. He favored a modernization of the educational curriculum, popular education, and temperance.[56] The reform movement in the South was eventually extinguished by the sentiment against abolition, which linked all support of change with the anti-slavery movement.

The literature of reform was well under way in America by the time White wrote *Modern Honor* in 1812. The Quaker John Woolman had attacked slavery in his *Journal* (1774), Brockden Brown, influenced by William Godwin and Mary Wollstonecraft, had championed the cause of women in a tract entitled *Alcuin; A Dialogue* (1798). In plays, Hannah Moore had advocated schools for women in *The Search for Happiness* (1794?) and Sarah Rowson had denounced all forms of slavery, including women's, in *Slaves in Algiers* (1794). Dueling was attacked incidentally in *The Better Sort* (1798), an anonyomus play in which a Yankee character says he considers dueling "anti-federal."[57] Josef Elfenbein finds, however, in plays from 1782 to 1812 that White's *Modern Honor* is the "only play of the period with the evils of dueling for a dominant thesis."[58] White may have known an English novel opposed to dueling, published in 1805, *The Duellists; or Men of Honour.*[59] Both authors use the term "honor" ironically.

It was appropriate that the first anti-dueling play should be written by a Southerner. In the era of the early republic, the custom was most prevalent in the South and especially in South Carolina and Georgia.[60] Charleston, in fact, "was conspicuous for the number of its duels" from the Revolution to the decade after the Civil War. The code of honor became more inexorable than any civil or moral law. Any man wanting to be regarded a gentleman conformed, or he suffered contempt from the high and low. Despite lone voices of protest crying in the wilderness, this sentiment persisted for a long time.[61] Some of the most prominent statesmen of the South supported the code by precept and example; among them were Henry Clay, John Randolph of Roanoke, and Andrew Jackson.[62]

General Charles Cotesworth Pinckney stands out as the most notable supporter of the anti-dueling movement in the early nineteenth century. He was so shocked by the death of Hamilton in 1804 that he used his great personal influence as president of the Society of Cincinnati to oppose the practice.[63] Although frequent laws and sermons show the opposition to dueling in the South,[64] the practice retained its vigor. In 1809 Georgia passed a law against dueling, and in 1810 Virginia approved an ordinance, but it had no more force than the Georgia law.[65] South Carolina passed an act in December, 1812, the same year as White's play, prescribing punishment and exclusion from the professions, trade, and public office for principals and seconds in a duel. This law also failed in its purpose.[66]

White mentions dueling several times in his journal. On August 21, 1817, he lamented the death of a friend in a duel, Dennis O'Driscoll, whose sister became his wife two years later. He wrote that the condition of the bereaved wife and parents showed "the fatal effects of this hateful practice of Dueling."[67]

Modern Honor was first performed at the Charleston Theatre on March 6, 9, and 12, 1812.[68] It presents the moral very forcefully in the brief life of the impetuous young Woodville. This tragedy in blank verse with an unspecified setting involves the machinations of the villain Forsythe to win Maria, the betrothed of Woodville, for himself. First, he implants a suspicion of Woodville's immorality in the minds of Maria and her brother, Charles Devalmore. He reminds them that Woodville has just returned from Europe, where morals are lax. Next, in the fashion of Iago, he raises the question of Maria's fidelity in Woodville's mind. With Woodville watching, he has his henchman, Flaurence, climb a ladder to Maria's window, in a scene that recalls the deception practiced

by Borachio on Claudio in *Much Ado About Nothing* (III.iii).
Devalmore sees the man at the window also and thinks he is Woodville. Later, he finds Forsythe embracing Maria and mistakes him
for Woodville. For the sake of his sister's honor, Devalmore duels
Woodville but is killed. He is mourned by his wife, Caroline, whose
name perhaps suggests the women of Carolina whose husbands have
died in duels. In the end, Woodville meets Forsythe in a duel. Hanmer, Woodville's second, pleads with Woodville to replace "modern
honor" with true honor, but he cannot stop his friend from going
to his death. It is interesting to note that at the first performance,
Forsythe was depicted as a military officer. A correspondent to the
Charleston *Times* (March 12, 1812) wrote that some of the audience had objected to this point even though not all members of
that class were meant. He reported that the author, not wanting "to
wound the feelings of a single honest man," had changed Forsythe
to a plain citizen in the next performance.[69]

Arguments are presented for dueling by the villains and against
the custom by Hanmer. Forsythe declares that the pistol has "more
civilized the world / Than all the pratings of your grizly sages." In
fact, it brings peace by the severe penalty it imposes on him who
"wages causeless strife." Flaurence remarks that it is hardly necessary to argue in favor of dueling since "the foremost characters in
all our land" uphold its usefulness (II.i). On the other hand, Hanmer attacks "sanctioned murder." In a soliloquy on the dueling
grounds, he exclaims:

Will no immortal patriot arise
Inspired with legislative energy,
To drive her from the land . . . !   (V. i)

Although this work will strike the modern reader as implausible
and ludicrous at times with its deep-dyed villains and stilted language, it possesses merits and marks an improvement over White's
first two plays. The tight construction of the drama and the hot

tempers of Woodville, Devalmore, and Forsythe give an impetus to the plot. White maintains the unity of time, as well as place and action; Woodville's return and death extend only from one morning to the next. The death of Devalmore occurs off stage, and thus does not detract from the duel of Woodville and Forsythe, the actual climax of the play which takes place on stage. Finally, the thematic conflicts are very clear: reason and passion vie for dominance within Woodville while arguments for and against dueling rage around him. The solutions indicated are Reason, Religion, and Legislation instead of dueling and "modern honor."

White noted that his play received "the utmost applause" on the first night. He was not as satisfied with attendance at the next two performances since the third night, for his benefit, did not "clear the expences."[70] It is possible that the support enjoyed by dueling took its toll at the theatre box office. A writer for the Charleston *Times* (March 6, 1812) commented on *Modern Honor* and the influence of the theatre. He stated that the pulpit denunciations of dueling had been in vain. The best argument is to show that dueling is not sanctioned "by magnanimity," or "the opinions of the world." He believed that the theatre could accomplish this goal best.

A second movement joined by White was the campaign against capital punishment, which obtained widespread support in the 1830's and '40's. Before the Literary and Philosophical Society on July 14, 1834, he delivered "An essay on the Moral Effect and tendency of Capital Punishment, and upon the propriety of substituting punishments of a milder nature."[71] Later a part of this essay entitled "The Dungeon and the Gallows" was printed in *The Charleston Book,* edited by William Gilmore Simms. The execution of a man and a women served to make the author's case against capital punishment. White wrote that to depict justly the horrors of this execution would require the pen of "a Maturin, a Byron, or a Scott." When the executioner was summoned, he rose from the floor of his cell "growling like some glutted hyena at being roused from his lair." As the woman went to her death, she shrieked and then made hurried prayers at the last. White does not ask that crimes go unpunished, but that "milder punishments" should take the place of death. He states that even the "vilest culprit" is a fellow being capable of repentance, but that is impossible after death, which seals the destiny of all.[72]

The third reform that White supported was temperance. For this cause he composed *The Forgers* in 1829.[73] Three years before, the parent organization of the movement had been formed. In 1836, one year before *The Forgers* was published, the American Temperance Union gave its sanction "to prose fiction and other 'light' literature as propaganda material for the movement." Short fiction advocating temperance appeared thereafter in great abundance during the late thirties.[74] The best-known temperance plays, however, did not reach the stage until later. *The Drunkard,* the greatest of these plays, started performances in 1844, and *Ten Nights in a Bar-Room* began in 1858.[75] Since White's play was composed in 1829 and printed in 1837, it stands as one of the first temperance plays.

According to David D. Wallace, it is difficult to realize the curse which intemperance laid on every class, including ministers, in South Carolina during this period. Iu 1828, Judge William D. James was removed for gross habitual drunkenness, sometimes extending through entire terms of court. This concern with drunkenness in the judiciary coincided with the temperance movement then beginning.[76]

According to Clement Eaton, the one "ism" that attained wide popularity in the antebellum South was the temperance movement because "it harmonized with the religious and puritanical feeling of many Southern people."[77] In 1829 the South Carolina Temperance Society was formed, and in the following years influential leaders in the state supported the movement. Thomas S. Grimké and Robert Barnwell Rhett were active in Charleston.[78] In 1836 Governor George McDuffie urged legislation to abolish liquor shops in Columbia because they corrupted college students. He was so little heeded, Judge Belton O'Neall said, that in 1857 there were sixty-four grog shops and only sixty-two temperance men in the city.[79] In time a connection between abolitionism and temperance was suspected in the South because such leading abolitionists as William Lloyd Garrison were temperance men, and from about 1834 on the temperance cause in the South declined.[80]

On August 9, 1836, White presented an "Address Delivered . . . at the Request of the Young Men's Temperance Society."[81] He advised abstinence, stating that " 'taste not, touch not,' is the only maxim of sound wisdom." Also, he expressed support of legislative action: "The Legislature should at once declare Intemperance to be a crime, and define punishments due its demerits." A writer in the *Courier* of August 12, 1836, opposed his proposal for legislative action. Parts of White's speech show similarities with his temperance play *The Forgers*. In the former, White refers to "the frightful effects of mania a potu" (madness from lack of wine) and quotes "Dr. Dickson," who says the victim is "perturbed with bad and disturbing dreams." In the last scene of the play the young victim of intemperance, Mordaunt, suffers from this condition and has hallucinations. Furthermore, in the address White asks dramatically what piercing shriek was that heard in the night and answers that it was a mother despairing of her "abandoned son." At the end of the play, Mordaunt's mother screams off stage as her son dies in prison.

The Forgers, a tragedy in blank verse, depicts the fall of young Mordaunt, whose numerous weaknesses are exploited by his false friend. The evil Ridgeford seeks Mordaunt's money and ruin because Laura, whom he had desired, is to become the bride of Mordaunt. Ridgeford is aided in his revenge by his sister, Coelestina, who had been in love with Mordaunt. When Mordaunt needs money, which his father now refuses him, Ridgeford persuades him to forge a check by signing the name of Fenton, Laura's wealthy father. Full of remorse for this deed, Mordaunt seeks advice from his friend Wardlaw, who advises him to confess and rely on the mercy of Laura and Fenton. Ridgeford rejects this advice saying that Wardlaw loves Laura. In Act IV, Scene 2, Mordaunt, "flushed with drink," accuses Laura of giving her love to Wardlaw and rushes out. A noise is heard off stage; Mordaunt has shot Wardlaw and believes that he has killed him. It is revealed later, however, that Ridgeford handed him a pistol and then killed Wardlaw himself by stabbing him. In prison, Mordaunt, suffering from lack of liquor, has hallucinations. He exclaims: "The walls are wrapped in flames! All is on fire!" He also sees forms that "revel in the flames / Hooting and shouting as they sweep along!" Ridgeford, in an adjoining cell, gives him a vial of poison, which he takes, thinking it liquor. He dies wracked with convulsions in the presence of his father and Fenton. The setting of this play is not named in the printed version but in the manuscript the following is written: "Scene, in any City of the United States, where Brandy, Whiskey, Wine, etc. etc. are freely drunk."

Ridgeford, like Fauresco in *The Mysteries of the Castle*, is another romantic villain whose evil schemes make him a forceful character. Speaking of his power over Mordaunt, he declares that it is he

Who tempts him, day by day, to drain the cup,
And add intemperance to his other crimes.   (I.i)

Like Forsythe in *Modern Honor*, he expresses opinions which White wished to condemn. Defending gambling, he says to Mordaunt:

Why gambling is the soul of trade, these days.
Without it, what is life? A desert waste.
The world itself's but one wide gambling board.

Next, when Mordaunt speaks of accepting the judgment of the law, Ridgeford sneers: "Law I do detest: / The scourge of innocence, the reward of guilt" (III.ii).

White's characterization of Mordaunt's parents is perceptive since they reveal themselves as contributors to their son's dissipation. Mrs. Mordaunt is an indulgent mother. When Mordaunt refuses to tell his father how he spends his money, she defends him, saying "a noble soul like his disdains" to give an account of "each cent he spends" (I.ii). At the end of this scene she consoles her son after Mr. Mordaunt has refused him another draft: "What would I not, to give that bosom rest!" In contrast, Mr. Mordaunt has not given enough attention to his son. He admits to Fenton that his business kept him too much from home. When he did turn to his son, he found Mordaunt's heart "possessed / And even rifled by intruder's hands!" Fenton observes:

> How oft our children's vices may we trace
> From seeds, by our own hands, in early life,
> With needless folly sown.   (III.iii)

In the next act, Mr. Modaunt reproaches himself again for not correcting his son:

> And had I chastened my beloved son,
> As Heaven in mercy now chastises me;
> I had not been this day abandoned thus.   (IV.ii)

White stated in a letter to "Dana" dated August 16, 1830,[82] that he planned to submit this tragedy to William Pelby's prize-play contest.[83] The play did not win the prize, and no record of a performance exists. In this letter, White's lengthy analysis of his play and comments on writing indicate that he strove to follow high standards. After saying that his work on the meter of the verse had extended over a considerable period, he remarked, "Time, I find to be absolutely essential to the due correction of any work of taste."

In introducing The Forgers to readers, the editor of the Southern Literary Journal made an interesting statement about the originality of White's drama. In most previous dramatic works, intemperance had been treated "with levity." Furthermore, the hero had appeared often as "one worthy of imitation rather than pity, abhorrence, or aversion." The editor concluded: "Indeed, this is the first time, we believe, that the Dramatic Poet has given the subject exclusively his attention and treated it after a grave and serious manner, although one most prolific of incident and capable of producing highly tragical effects."[34]

A major fault in this play is the lack of unity. The title shifts the emphasis from the main vice, intemperance, to forging. Also, the revenge motif detracts from unity since the evil machinations of Ridgeford play as important a part in Mordaunt's downfall as intemperance. Despite these errors, White showed again in this play that by blending social concern with romantic scenes and characters, he could produce a work of dramatic force.

A Political Play:
The Triumph of Liberty

The Triumph of Liberty, or Louisiana Preserved is a historical drama with a political purpose.[85] White's play celebrates, first, Jackson's great victory in the War of 1812. The event had already been dramatized by C. E. Grice in The Battle of New Orleans (1815). In later years this battle was treated often, for example, by G. W. P. Custis in The Eighth of January (1831). The major purpose of The Triumph of Liberty, however, is to defend Jackson's actions during the Seminole War of 1818, after which Florida was ceded to the United States. As already shown in Ioor's Battle of Eutaw Springs, an earlier event may provide the vehicle for commenting on a contemporary situation. These works, along with Ioor's Independence and James Workman's Liberty in Louisiana, discussed above, demonstrate that a close scrutiny of many early American plays combined with an alertness to events occurring at the time of composition would uncover the immediate political purposes of the dramatists.[86]

In the months before White finished The Triumph of Liberty in

August, 1818, newspapers were filled with reports of Jackson's Seminole War and the trials of Alexander Arbuthnot and Robert C. Ambrister, two British citizens serving as agents of the Indians. His inclusion of two characters named Arbuthnot and Ambrister in scenes with the Indians makes clear that the play deals with the Seminole War as well as the War of 1812.

A brief account of the events leading up to the trials of Arbuthnot and Ambrister will provide the basis for understanding fully White's play. In 1817 a number of incidents occurred along the Georgia-Florida border that eventually led to Jackson's Seminole War. The United States charged that Spain had not kept the Indians from depredating north of the line. Some settlers had been killed by Indians, and Americans had also taken lives in attacks. When the Seminole chiefs declined a conference at Fort Scott, Georgia, the Indian border village of Fowltown was burned in retaliation by Americans. The Seminoles in return ambushed an American hospital ship on the Appalachicola River, killing thirty-four soldiers, seven women, and four children. In view of the foregoing events and his belief that Spanish Florida posed a threat to the Mississippi Valley, Jackson led his Tennessee Volunteers into the territory in March, 1818. On April 6, 1818, he took the fort at St. Mark's and captured Alexander Arbuthnot. In the harbor, Captain McKeever changed his American flag to British and deceived on board his ship the Seminole prophet Francis (also called Hillis Hadjo) and Chief Homollimico. Both were hanged summarily. At Chief Bowleck's village on the Suwannee, Jackson captured Lieutenant Robert C. Ambrister, late of the British Royal Marines, and discovered documents convincing him that Ambrister and Arbuthnot were at the bottom of the Seminole disturbances. At the military court held at St. Mark's April 26-28, 1818, Arbuthnot was accused of inciting the Indians to war and acting as a spy. Ambrister was charged with aiding the enemy and levying war against the United States. They were found guilty and executed.[87] It is this part of the war that is pertinent to White's play since it contains scenes showing Arbuthnot and Ambrister conniving with the Indians.

Jackson's proceedings in Florida provoked strong disapproval in some quarters and an emotional debate in Congress. The English press denounced him, and there was talk of war, but Lord Castlereagh opposed such sentiments with firmness.[88] Not since the trial of Aaron Burr had America's interest been so captured.[89] Henry Clay made a speech in the House on January 8, 1819, which was critical of Jackson; he opposed allowing "unlimited discretion in our military commanders."[90] In February, 1819, when President Monroe sent to the Senate the treaty ceding Florida, a House committee submitted a report disapproving the executions and other actions of Jackson; it was defeated.[91] A report from Abner Lacock's committee to the Senate was also very disapproving, but it was not acted upon. In the autumn of 1819, John Overton completed under Jackson's supervision a defense of the Seminole War. This memorial was presented in the Senate on February 23, 1820, and here the affair ended.[92]

During the Congressional debate on Jackson's conduct in Florida, the Charleston *Courier* supported the condemnation of Jackson. Its strong stand shows that the question was controversial in Charleston and provides the best explanation of why *The Triumph of Liberty*, which defended Jackson's execution of Arbuthnot and Ambrister, was not performed at the Charleston Theatre. On January 7, 1819, the *Courier* printed an article from the New York *Daily Advertiser* condemning Jackson's execution of two Indians. On January 15, 1819, the *Courier* reprinted from the Richmond *Enquirer* a long attack by "Algernon Sidney" on the secretary of state, John Quincy Adams, for defending Jackson in his letter to the United States minister in Madrid. In the *Courier* January 25, 1819, a Washington correspondent said that in the debate Jackson has many supporters and he fears he will be in a minority, for I am "under the same banners as yourself." A few years however will set things right and "justify our opinions." The Editors of the *Courier* added: "Of this last opinion we have no doubt." In this dislike of Jackson, we can see the lingering antipathy of the Federalists to the popular Republican leader. As the *Courier* chastised Jefferson before, it later found fault with Jackson.

White published *The Triumph of Liberty* on May 3, 1819, after the debates in Congress, but while the controversy was still continuing. It is noteworthy that the play appeared on the last day of President James Monroe's visit to Charleston. White met the president on this occasion and also Major-General Edmund P. Gaines, who had presided at the court-martial of Arbuthnot and Ambrister. It is possible that the two visitors saw copies of this play. White wrote that James H. Caldwell, the famous actor, promised to stage *The Triumph of Liberty* at his Petersburg, Virginia, theatre, but no record of its performance has been found.[93] The best conjecture for its omission at the Charleston Theatre seems to be the controversial nature of the Seminole War and opposition to Jackson, such as that expressed by the influential *Courier.*

The Triumph of Liberty presents as its principal plot the Battle of New Orleans. Before the engagement, Jackson discusses fortifications and the civic affairs of Louisiana with his inspector general and Governor William C. C. Claiborne. Some citizens called Tories sow discord and inform the British of American preparations. The British under Sir Edward Pakenham are villainous with their watchword of "Booty and Beauty" (V.i). Much of the action of the battle in Acts IV and V is reported by characters, but in Act V, Scene 2, after Jackson has spoken words of encouragement, the militiamen form lines on stage and fire. A young Kentuckian, Jonathan Staunchford, shoots General Pakenham. This scene bears an interesting resemblance to White's painting, *The Battle of New Orleans.* A description in the *Courier* (August 5, 1816) says that in the painting "the Kentucky Militia Riflemen are firing upon the enemy." In the center appears "Gen. Packenham falling from his horse." Jackson and his officers "are surveying the scene" from the ramparts. At the end of the play, Jackson responds graciously to the praise of children and the Abbé Dubourg, Administrator Apostolic of the Catholic Diocese of Louisiana.[94]

The first subplot involves two fictional families. Delancy, a Tennessee farmer, sees his son Virginius go off to join his regiment after the British have burned Washington. His daughter, Carolina, is kidnapped by the Indians. In a scene reflecting White's penchant for the Gothic, she is taken to a skull-lined cavern to be sacrificed, but is saved by Jonathan Staunchford, disguised as an Indian. The Staunchford and Delancy families arrive together in New Orleans before the battle. Another fictional subplot presents a sailor Heartwell, who had been held in the British prison at Dartmoor, England, but has now returned to America. He is reunited with his wife, Orliana, and their children. The names "Carolina," "Virginius," and "Orliana," like "Caroline" in *Modern Honor*, are appropriate and obviously symbolic. Many settlers in Tennessee were from Virginia and the Carolinas, and Jackson benefited them and the inhabitants of New Orleans by his victories in the War of 1812 and the Seminole War.

The scenes involving the Indians form the most significant part of this play because they reveal the author's interest in the Seminole War (Scenes 2-5 of Act I and all of Act III). White is not concerned with historical accuracy since the Seminole War occurred three years after the Battle of New Orleans. His objective is to confirm the charge that Arbuthnot and Ambrister incited the Seminoles against the Americans, thus justifying Jackson in their execution. He carries out this purpose in the following scenes. In Act I, Scene 2, Arbuthnot and Ambrister bring trinkets to the Red-stick chiefs and to Mickadekoa, a Seminole chief. They promise that the British king, George III, will send forces to defeat the Americans. Chief Tookaubatcha, then, invites them to see the prophet Hillis Hadjo. At a council fire Arbuthnot and Ambrister meet the prophet and bring with them weapons. They again promise that the British king will overcome the Americans, and the Indians praise "Great George!" At the end of the scene the two Britons urge the Indians to attack the Americans, saying, "Exterminate!" (III.i) By presenting Arbuthnot and Ambrister as arming the Indians and inciting them to kill Americans, White was following the conclusions of the court martial. Arbuthnot was convicted of urging war against the United States and inciting the Indians to kill two American traders. The prosecution showed that he had given the Indians ten kegs of powder. Evidence was presented also that Ambrister gave ammunition to the Indians.[95]

The following points show clearly that White is concerned with the Seminole War in the Indian scenes and not with the Battle of New Orleans. First, neither Arbuthnot nor Ambrister took part in the War of 1812. Arbuthnot did not come to Florida until 1817.[96] Ambrister also arrived after the Battle of New Orleans.[97] Second, Hillis Hadjo, the prophet, also called Francis, was not involved in the War of 1812. His name became prominent after the Battle of New Orleans when he was taken to London by Colonel Edward Nicholls, a British officer, who negotiated a military alliance with the Florida Indians.[98] When Jackson invaded Florida in 1818, Hillis Hadjo went to the ship flying the British flag in St. Mark's harbor and was hanged by the Americans.[99] In the play, this reliance on Great Britain is brought out by the Indians' eager acceptance of the promises made by Arbuthnot and Ambrister. Third, in the Seminole War as in the play, the Seminole and Red-stick chiefs made common cause. After the Creek War, some Red-sticks went to Florida and joined the Seminoles, who were also part of the Creek nation.[100] Nine Seminole and three Red-Stick chiefs gave Arbuthnot power of attorney to represent them in any business whatsoever.[101] Fourth, the mutual attacks made by Americans and Seminoles that led to the war are represented by those described in the play. When trouble broke out in 1817, it would be hard to say who was responsible. The Seminoles, for instance, complained that Americans had slain ten of their people and owed them three, meaning that they themselves had killed seven Americans.[102] In the play, the Indian chiefs complain to Arbuthnot that the Americans kill "our squaws and children" (I.ii). Shortly afterward, however, the Red-Sticks kidnap Carolina Delancy, thus showing the kind of attacks suffered by the Americans (I.v).[103]

Though there is criticism of Jackson in the play, it is greatly outweighed by praise. After the general has declared martial law in New Orleans, two Tories, M'Craig and Arundale, denounce him before Pakenham: "The Military Despot, usurps authority! He drags our citizens into the ranks" (V.i.). This reference to military harshness was the same being expressed in the Seminole Affair. The praise of Jackson is lavish. His civilian, as well as his military, virtues are emphasized in the play. Farmer Delancy describes him to his son: "Behold in him, the gentleman and the scholar, the statesman, the patriot, the soldier, and the hero: to make his character complete, the steady, stern, inflexible Republican" (I.i).

White's defense of Jackson in *The Triumph of Liberty* and his two reform plays demonstrate that his strong concern with American topics, seen in his political opinions and paintings, extended to his dramas. Critics of his plays like Ludwig Lewisohn and Arthur Hobson Quinn have erroneously stressed his works with foreign settings; they have completely disregarded his shift to American issues.[104] This progression toward American subjects makes White more than just another writer of foreign plays. Through his works about dueling, intemperance, and Andrew Jackson, he represents clearly the desire in the new republic to deal seriously in drama with the principal issues confronting the American people. His writing emphasizes this aspect of early nineteenth century Charleston plays: the direct relationship to pressing concerns of the day.

V

WILLIAM GILMORE SIMMS

illiam Gilmore Simms (1806-1870) provides a fitting conclusion to the tradition of writing for the Charleston theatre. Although Simms's best writing is his fiction, he was greatly interested in composing plays and wrote a sizeable number in his lifetime. He illustrates best the condition of playwriting for the Charleston theatre during the period from 1826 to 1860. Simms succeeded in getting only one of his plays performed, *Michael Bonham,* in 1855, twelve years after it was composed. He however continued the tradition of the theatre as a political platform, as evidenced by his two most significant plays, *Michael Bonham* (for the annexation of Texas) and *Norman Maurice* (for the admission of new slave states in the West).

The tradition of dramatic writing in Charleston is an important part of Simms's background. As the theological and historical writing in New England served as a milieu from which emerged the trancendentalism of Emerson and the fiction of Hawthorne, so a tradition of writing lay behind Simms in Charleston. This tradition includes historical writing (like Dr. David Ramsay's *History*

WILLIAM GILMORE SIMMS.
COURTESY, SOUTH CAROLINIANA LIBRARY.

of South Carolina), journals (like the *Southern Review,* edited by Hugh Swinton Legaré), and belles-lettres (like the witty *vers de société* of William Crafts, seen in "The Raciad" and "Sullivan's Island"). This background, however, is incomplete without the addition of dramatic writing done by such men as William Ioor and John Blake White. Some of the earlier dramatic composition had a clear connection with Simms's Revolutionary romances. The glorification of the Revolution, which also appeared in historical writing and painting, occurred in the numerous pageants like Placide's *The Attack on Fort Moultrie* (1794) and in Ioor's *Battle of Eutaw Springs* (1807).

The importance of drama in Simms's career is quite evident. Simms's two main writings on drama concerned Shakespeare. He considered his best study "The Moral Character of Hamlet" (1844), a long essay in several parts, which he delivered as a lecture at the Smithsonian Institute.[1] In this analysis, he compared Hamlet to an unsuccessful, irresolute gentleman in another old civilization, that of Charleston. In 1848 he published *A Supplement to the Plays of William Shakespeare.* This volume begins with a long introduction in which Simms theorizes on Shakespeare's apprenticeship as a dramatist and contains apocryphal plays like *Locrine* and *Sir John Oldcastle* with introductions by Simms.

The influence of drama on Simms's fictional technique appears particularly in his characterization. The psychology found in Elizabethan and Restoration plays influenced Simms's presentation of the humors and passions. Surgeon Hillhouse in *The Scout* delights in clothing as does Sir Fopling Flutter in George Etherege's *The Man of Mode.* Porgy thinks of eating perpetually and Millhouse's humor in *Woodcraft* is practicality when he advises Porgy on the useful.[2]

Parallels between Shakespearean scenes and characters and Simms's are numerous and demonstrate the influence. Porgy is likened to Falstaff in the Revolutionary novels. He has a big belly and in *Katharine Walton* calls for a drink from Lance Frampton much as Falstaff does from Prince Hal in *Henry IV*, Part 1. The wild, Macbeth-like imagination is seen in *Richard Hurdis* in the visions of Pickett. In *Border Beagles*, Horsey the Shakespearean actor, is full of dramatic poesy, like Pistol.³ A favorite quote from Shakespeare was "Othello's occupation's gone," which Simms used in *Woodcraft*.⁴ Othello is a source for the jealous husband in *Confession*.

Simms's knowledge of drama influenced his fundamental fictional theory as seen in his comparison of the drama to the romance in the preface to *The Yemassee*. Simms wrote that the standards are much the same for the drama and the romance. The action of both occurs in "a narrow space of time"; both require the "same unities of plan, of purpose and harmony of parts."⁵ Simms's writing and attending plays also must have contributed to his handling of exciting theatrical climax, evident in the siege of the Block House in *The Yemassee*.

Simms and the Charleston Theatre

Simms had a long and close relationship with the Charleston theatre. He not only wrote plays designed for the Charleston stage, but he also supported it through opening addresses, theatrical criticism, and an account of dramatists for the Charleston theatre. Dr. John B. Irving noted that Simms wrote inaugural addresses for two Charleston theatres. He wrote that twice in "sweetest numbers" Simms announced the opening of a new theater, first in Meeting Street and second in "King-street."⁶ The first was for the New Charleston Theatre in 1837, and the next was for the theatre built in 1869, the Academy of Music.⁷

When the New Charleston Theatre was about to open in 1837 Simms gave some advice. He wrote that the failure of the theatre in America had resulted from managers' attempting to make it "democratic." They had required the muses to perform for the vulgar. The price of a theatre ticket should be the same in all parts of the house, but a good one. Theatrical companies should be "limited, but select." A small stock company, each of whom knows his place, will be well supported, but the public will not pay for "stars which shine for a few nights only." Simms also implied that the theatre had its share of low life in the audience. Trouble from this group could be avoided by a large overhead light.[8] When the New Theatre opened in 1837, it had a large chandelier to illuminate all of the seats.[9]

After the Civil War when Simms was trying to encourage reverence for previous accomplishments, he wrote a lengthy article for the *XIX Century* called "Our Early Authors and Artists" in which he served as historian for the dramatists of the Charleston theatre. In his comments on John Blake White he discussed his paintings and dramas. On his paintings, he wrote that White's "design and groupings were . . . really spirited and good. His *finish* was not held in the same esteem."[10] Simms had shown an earlier interest in White's paintings in a reference to his canvas *Battle of Fort Moultrie* in the opening paragraphs of a story, "Battle of Fort Moultrie." The painting, he said, had merits because it kept a hold on his "senses."[11] In 1840 he asked James Lawson in New York to buy for him an engraving of White's *Camp of Marion*.[12] On White's plays, Simms wrote that several were produced at an early date at the Charleston Theatre, written generally in blank verse. His *Foscari* was "certainly not a great deal worse than that of Lord Byron, written on the same subject."[13]

Simms's comment on William Ioor and his *Battle of Eutaw Springs* is especially noteworthy. He wrote in 1869 that he met Ioor nearly forty years ago on a deer hunt in St. Paul's parish when the "venerable author" was then fully seventy years of age. Ioor had the good luck to "get the shot, and the skill to drop the buck on the instant, in his tracks." Simms then recalls that he owned a copy of Ioor's drama, *The Battle of Eutaw Springs,* but lost it; this was "among the first if not the very first, native dramas brought on the boards." The success of the play, however, was "due rather to its patriotism than to his literary execution."[14]

In the next installment of "Our Early Authors and Artists," Simms stated that while he was confessing his deficiency because of the loss of Ioor's play, "Dublin University Magazine" supplied a review.[15] After quoting the British critic's summary of the acts and his attacks on the faults of Ioor's play, Simms stated that "if our memory serves us rightly" the critic has been "guilty of the *suppressio veri*." He said that "certainly our critic has suppressed some of the incidents of the drama which would have told successfully." He then gave "a matter of history," that is, an actual historical incident which a comedian could have made effective. In the play, Lt. Manning, fleeing from the brick house at Eutaw placed little Major Barry, Judge Advocate of the British Army, on his shoulders and used him as a shield from the British gunfire. Barry demanded that he be set down since he was "Major Barry, Judge Advocate of the British Army." Manning refused, answering that Barry was "the very handsome person I have been loking after." Simms says "this ludicrous scene was necessarily very successful with the groundlings." He concludes, "Our critic tells us nothing of this and some other things which were in the play, and, no doubt, reconciled the audience to its absurdities."[16] In his accounts of "Our Early Authors," Simms also commented on the plays of Isaac Harby, Edwin C. Holland, William Crafts, and William Elliot.[17]

Simms as Dramatist

Simms composed plays from a very early age to almost the end of his life. Although he succeeded much better in fiction, he showed progress in dramaturgy. He wrote primarily as a literary man and not as a professional dramatist. His many unsuccessful efforts to get plays performed are in marked contrast to the ease with which he published fiction. In his dramatic career, Simms had dealings mainly with his literary agent, James Lawson; Edwin Forrest, the famous actor; and two managers at the Charleston Theatre, W. C. Forbes and F. C. Adams.

Simms's earliest dramatic writings extended from about 1825 to 1835 and consisted of dramatic poems and sketches. His earliest dramatic composition was a tragedy written when he was about eighteen. This verse drama presented Pelayo, the legendary founder of Spain, in his struggle against Roderick, the tyrant Goth.[18] Simms later converted this play into two novels: *Pelayo* (1839) and *Count Julian, or the Last of the Goths* (1845). In 1832 Simms published a dramatic poem "Atalantis." This is a fanciful piece about water nymphs and a shipwrecked Spanish sailor. Drawing from his early writings Simms published later several dramatic fragments. James W. Dewsnap conjectures that these early dramatic sketches were written between 1825 and 1835.[19] Among them are the following: "Blondeville," *Southern Literary Messenger,* (June, 1837); "Sylla, the Dictator," *Southern Literary Journal,* (September, 1838); "Pelayo" (a fragment from the earlier play which he converted into two novels), *The Rambler,* published in Charleston (November-December, 1843); "The Death of Cleopatra," *Graham's Magazine* (December, 1849), republished in "Historical Legends," in *Poems, Descriptive, Dramatic, Legendary, and Contemplative* (1853); "Caius Marius," *Graham's Magazine* (January, 1850) and in *Poems;* "Bertram," *Graham's Magazine* (July, 1851), also in *Poems*; "The Passage of the Red Sea," part of the novel *Pelayo* (published in the *Charleston Mercury* October 14, 1863); and "The Bitter Feud," in *Southern Field and Fireside* (January, 1846).[20]

In the summer of 1832, Simms met Forrest through his agent James Lawson, a good friend of the actor.[21] Forrest was the catalyst for Simms to start writing plays designed for acting as well as publication. For three decades Simms tried unsuccessfully to get Forrest to act in a play. A few months after meeting Forrest, Simms wrote Lawson that he was thinking of preparing "my tragedy for Forrest, who asked me to do so."[22] At this time Forrest was the leading advocate for Americans to write plays. He sponsored nine playwriting contests with monetary prizes from 1828 to

EDWIN FORREST, FRIEND OF SIMMS, AS SPARTACUS IN
The Gladiator. HE PLAYED THIS ROLE IN CHARLESTON,
JANUARY 18, 1841 AND FEBRUARY 3 AND 4, 1847.
COURTESY, HOBLITZELLE THEATRE ARTS COLLECTION
UNIVERSITY OF TEXAS.

1847.[23] Through Lawson, Simms invited Forrest to visit him at Woodlands in letters dated September 5, 1840 and September 15, 1840.[24] These were the first of such invitations; none were accepted.

In one of Simms's novels the author made a criticism of Forrest's acting that may have given offense. In *Border Beagles* (first published, 1841), Tom Horsey, the comical, aspiring young actor, imitates the "gutteral growl of Forrest."[25] Evidently Forrest and Lawson did not like this description because Simms wrote to Lawson in apparent apology that he considered Forrest "a great natural Genius" despite such defects as the growl which was in his voice at times.[26]

In the 1840's, the decade of Simms's greatest activity in playwriting, he continued trying to interest Forrest in his plays. In the summer of 1844, Simms wrote Lawson that he was bringing north his Texas drama (*Michael Bonham,* which W. C. Forbes had failed to produce in Charleston during the spring) for Forrest's perusal and that portion of his tragedy ("Don Carlos") that he had submitted to William Charles Macready, the English actor.[27] At this time Forrest was involved in his disputes with Macready which finally resulted in the Astor Place riot of 1849 and would not have approved Simms's submission of a play to Macready.

During this decade Simms began two plays for Forrest which he did not finish and which remain in manuscript: "Don Carlos" and "The Death of the British Brutus," an adaptation of *Locrine,* the apocryphal Shakespearean play. The first play portrays the son of Philip II and resembles Schiller's *Don Carlos* (translation published in 1836).[28] Simms had published *Locrine* in *A Supplement to the Plays of William Shakespeare* (1848). In April, 1851, he published his adaptation of this play as "The Death of the British Brutus; a Dramatic Sketch" in *Sartain's Magazine.*[29] This is the first extant example of Simms's attempt to adapt Shakespeare for the nineteenth century stage.[30] Earlier, Simms had written Lawson on November 18, 1846, that he was considering submitting his adaptation of *Locrine* to Forbes.[31]

Simms's major effort to write a play to Forrest's liking was *Norman Maurice; or, The Man of the People*. On September 5, 1847, he wrote Lawson that he hoped to finish this tragedy, which was composed for Forrest and based on his personality.[32] Forrest was cool to the idea.[33] Becoming impatient with Forrest, Simms wrote Lawson to persuade Forrest to read the last act of *Norman Maurice*. If he did not like it, he would make "a volume of my Arnold, Michael Bonham, Locrine, Atalantis, & adding this 'man of the people', close my account with the Dramatic World in a single publication."[34] In 1853, Simms partially executed this plan by collecting *Norman Maurice*, "Atalantis," and some dramatic sketches in his *Poems, Descriptive, Dramatic, Legendary, and Contemplative*.[35] On November 20, 1848, Simms wrote Lawson that he had seen the actor James Murdoch in Charleston and in the event Forrest did not take "The Man of the People" Lawson was to place it in Murdoch's hands.[36] Simms finally published *Norman Maurice* in 1850; it appeared thereafter in six editions, but was never performed. In 1852, Simms wrote F. C. Adams of the Charleston Theatre in an effort to get it produced there.

In the 1850's Simms continued his dramatic efforts with some waning of energy. Through a letter from F. C. Adams, he was asked in 1852 by James D. B. DeBow, editor of *DeBow's Review*, to dramatize his novelette *The Golden Christmas*, but Simms declined, saying he did not have the time. In turning down DeBow's request he wrote F. C. Adams that "dramatic writing, was my first literary passion, and I believe it to be my forte." He continued that he had several pieces on hand but had found the business unprofitable and unpleasant. Actors would not learn new pieces. He felt, however, the theatre could not succeed without new plays. "In Shakespeare's time," he said, "the rule with managers was to produce a new piece every tenth or twelfth night."[37]

"Timon of Athens," an adaptation of the Shakespearean play, was the last work Simms designed for Forrest.[38] Simms mentioned to Lawson on October 21, 1852, that he was writing "Timon of

Athens." By December 1, 1852, he had completed and sent it to Forrest but had not received a reply.[39] This play presents a former soldier in financial trouble who is seeking a wife. It was composed about the same time as *Woodcraft* and resembles this novel in plot, since *Woodcraft* is about the impecunious Captain Porgy seeking a wife after his return from the Revolutionary War. The novel was written in 1852[40] and first published serially in the *Southern Literary Gazette Supplement* (February-November, 1852).

In 1854 Simms was informed that *Norman Maurice* was being rehearsed in Nashville and would be produced in St. Louis, but this performance never occurred. In 1855 Simms's single play to be produced, *Michael Bonham,* was given at the Charleston Theatre as the benefit for the Calhoun Monument Association. Simms's last play to be published was "Benedict Arnold: The Traitor. A Drama, in an Essay." It appeared serially in the Richmond *Magnolia Weekly* (May 16-August 1, 1863). Simms had begun the drama in 1824.[41] In 1848 he wrote Lawson that he had given the rude draft of his dramatic poem "Benedict Arnold" to W. C. Forbes. The manager had requested to see it, and Simms desired his evaluation. The play was revised in 1862 before being finally published in 1863.[42]

Michael Bonham; or, The Fall of Bexar

Michael Bonham was composed originally to support the annexation of Texas, but when it was presented in 1855 its purpose was to support Simms's aim of finding a Southern political leader to replace Calhoun. It was presented as a benefit for the Calhoun Monument Association and Simms added an "Ode to Calhoun," which was read at the performance.

The progress of this play from composition through publication and performance took twelve years. Simms's first mention of *Michael Bonham* was in 1843. He wrote James Lawson on November 15, 1843, that he was preparing for Forbes a melodrama about the conquest of the Alamo and the subsequent battle of San Jacinto. He hoped to conclude the play that week.[43] Simms evidently informed Forrest about *Michael Bonham* because he received an encouraging letter about it on January 10, 1844, beginning "My dear Simms." Forrest was glad that Simms had employed himself in preparing a drama and regretted that "more of our American authors" do not apply themselves to that difficult purpose, the production of a successful play. He advised him that it would be "quite fair" for him to reserve "the rights of all interests" in his play "beyond the limits of Mr. Forbes' present circuit."[44]

Simms wrote Lawson on February 15, 1844, that the terms of his play with Forbes were not to be as he wrote to Forrest. Because of "the bungling terms" stated in the manager's letter he was only to get half the gross proceeds of the third night.[45] On March 8, 1844, Simms said his play was in the hands of the manager. It had been rehearsed twice, according to a letter from Forbes, and all things were ready. Simms was pessimistic about a performance, however, since the actors were taking their benefits, which was the sign of the close of the season. He stated that if he visited the city next week he might withdraw it from Forbes' hands.[46] On November 19, 1846, Simms wrote Lawson that he had again sent his Texan drama to Forbes, but whether he would play it or not was still a question. Simms had cut it considerably.[47] In November, 1847, he wrote Lawson that when he passed through Augusta he strolled to the theatre and talked to Forbes, who spoke of making "some alterations" and bringing out *Michael Bonham* there. Simms remarked, "Of course, I attach no importance to the matter now & let him do as he pleases."[48] The last comment probably means that since the plays' purpose, the annexation of Texas, had been accomplished in 1845, Simms had lost interest in a stage production.

Simms was still interested in putting himself "on the record," as he would say.[49] He first published *Michael Bonham* in *The Southern Literary Messenger* from February through June, 1852. It was next published in a separate volume in the fall of 1852 by John Reuben Thompson, a Richmond publisher and editor of the *Southern Literary Messenger*. A comparison of these two editions shows that they are the same. Simms stated in a short introduction that the play was first written for performance but he had since persuaded himself that it would read better "as a story." He further remarked that he had taken some liberty with the facts, but that history would suffer little and the story would gain thereby.[50] Simms did in fact take liberties since the man on whom the title character was based took no part in the siege of Bexar (San Antonio) from December 5 to 9, 1835. The historic person, James Butler Bonham, did not arrive until January or February, 1836, in San Antonio, where he died at the Battle of the Alamo.[51]

It is ironic that after Simms stopped his efforts at production, *Michael Bonham* was presented at the Charleston Theater on March 26, 27, and 28, 1855. An editorial in the *Courier* (March 26, 1855) gives important information as to why it was produced. The play served to support construction of the Calhoun Monument. The *Courier* stated that the gentlemen of the "Theatrical Association" had offered the proceeds of the second night to the "Ladies Calhoun Monument Association." Since the hero of the play and the author were natives, the *Courier* continued, the play should be patronized. Furthermore, the community should support the monument.

Although Simms did not attend a performance, on March 27, 1855, he wrote Evert Duyckinck that the play was performed "with great success." He said that if he was offered a benefit, he would attend, if only to get the money, which he needed. He then requested Duyckinck to ask his publisher, Julius Redfield, to publish the play as a separate volume for fifty cents.[52] This volume was never published, nor was Simms tendered a benefit performance. Simms complained to his friend Marcellus Hammond that the audience had not called for the author. Hammond asked in reply had that ever happened in "your goodly city." The audience, however, Hammond noted, paid Simms their highest compliment, "that of encoring scenes!" A song might do, but a scene, he said, "it is surely a *rara avis.*" After the play was performed, Hammond had seen M. L. Bonham, a hero of the Mexican War and brother of James Butler Bonham. He reported Bonham's reaction to the play: "Saw Bonham (M. L.) yesterday. His vanity is flattered. He was gratified at your success of which I told him."[53] On April 3, 1855, James H. Hammond, brother of Marcellus, congratulated Simms on the play's success and asked why he did not take a benefit. He asked if it was because of "your old morbidity."[54]

Michael Bonham was warmly reviewed in the Charleston newspapers. On March 26, 1855, the *Courier* printed a story on the front page entitled "Michael Bonham—Simms' Drama." It gave a synopsis of the play and remarked that Bonham was already known. He was a daring adventurer of the Palmetto State, an associate of Bowie, Davy Crockett, and that small band "who first planted" near the "Great River" of the American Spaniards the lone star flag. The *Courier* observed that one character, "Sparrow," was "a huge feeder and wit"; he seemed "a dramatic distillation of *Capt. Porgy,*" already a great favorite with all who had met him in Simms's Revolutionary novels.

On March 27, 1855, the *Courier* reported that the new drama by "our versatile and gifted *SIMMS*" was attended by a large audience, whose attention was shown by "frequent demonstrations of applause." The cast was good and "the general effect was more than creditable" for the first production. The advertisement of the play in this issue stated that it would conclude with an address written for the occasion by Simms and delivered by J. E. Nagle. This address was "Calhoun—An Ode." Nagle was an actor in the stock company and played the part of Michael Bonham.[55]

In the *Courier,* March 29, 1855, the Ladies' Calhoun Monument Association thanked Mr. John Sloman for his support of the play. Sloman was Acting Manager from October 30, 1854 to March 31,

1855.[56] His wife played Donna Olivia in the play, and he was Sparrow.[57]

The *Evening News* of March 27, 1855, praised *Michael Bonham,* but with some reservations. The critic commended the author for blending the passions of love and revenge, but said he suffered from "too great *nearness*" to the period in which he wrote. He said, nevertheless, that this work would prove "an acquisition to the stage," since it possessed a well-constructed plot and situations that form dramatic pictures. His main objection was to the comic relief, the character Sparrow. He wrote that Sparrow was modelled after Falstaff, but that his language was an expression of "grossness without piquancy to give it flavor." His dialogue should undergo "the process of excision."[58]

In the *Mercury* of March 29, 1855, the reviewer of *Michael Bonham* wrote that dramatic success is so rare in these times that the writer of a successful play is "a public benefactor." The stage both in England and the United States is beggared of such attractions. He seconds the *Evening News* by saying that the author should receive a benefit.[59]

Since *Michael Bonham* presents the Americans who later fell at the Alamo, it belongs with other plays that dealt with this battle. Arthur Hobson Quinn lists six plays about the Alamo from 1835 to 1839. For instance, "Fall of the Alamo; or, Texas and Her Oppressors," by an anonymous author, was produced at the Arch St. Theatre, Philadelphia, May 26, 1836.[60] None of these plays were published.

The main plot of *Michael Bonham* presents the Americans' entry into San Antonio (Bexar) in 1835, which immediately preceded the Battle of the Alamo. They are first camped outside the city, then enter, and at the end are installed in the Alamo. There is a romantic sub-plot. Michael Bonham (from the banks of the Congaree River in South Carolina), the young leader of the Americans, loves Donna Olivia, daughter of the cowardly, preposterous Mexican governor, Don Estaban. Maria, Olivia's cousin, also loves him but loses the contest and commits suicide at the end. Michael defeats his rival, Pedro, for Olivia in a sword fight. At the end Michael and Olivia are married in the Alamo. American characters represent different states: the fat Sparrow is from Georgia, Joe Kennedy and "Alabama" Davis from Alabama, and Davy Crockett from Tennessee.

The themes are simple and forceful. First, the Americans oppose Mexican tyranny and injustice. Olivia asks Michael if he is "a Texian rebel." He answers that he is a "Texian citizen," a friend of freedom, and rebellious against injustice (IV.vi).

The bravery of the Americans in fighting against the Mexicans is expressed by Joe Kennedy. He leads them in a song which proclaims that they are "soldiers of the north"; they have done battle with "old England" and can "smite." The refrain declares:

> We shall teach them that the bold,
> Still inherit all the fruits.
> And their moustaches and gold
> We shall pluck up by the roots.   (III.iii)

Another theme is the close relationship of Texas and the United States, obviously related to the purpose of annexation. When the fighting against the Mexicans begins, Michael Bonham tells his men:

> The old Thirteen, the great Southwest, the North,
> The Carolinas, Georgia, Tennessee,
> Countries of Bunker Hill and Saratoga,
> Cowpens and Eutaw, Moultrie's isle, Savannah,
> Are looking at your actions, as their sons,—
> They must not be dishonored.   (V.iii)

Michael Bonham is most significant for its political purpose, which demonstrates the Southern response on the stage to the antislavery movement. It is inaccurate to think that the Southern stage responded to the anti-slavery movement only through burlesques of such abolition plays as *Uncle Tom's Cabin.* In this play by Simms, the dramatist took the offensive by advocating the balancing of sectional power by the annexation of Texas. Its first aim, the annexation of Texas, which would be a slave-holding state, becomes clear when preceding historical events are set beside the date of composition, November, 1843. On March 6, 1836, occurred the Fall of the Alamo; soon afterward Sam Houston defeated Santa Anna at the Battle of San Jacinto on April 21, 1836, and Texas was proclaimed an independent republic. In the following years Texas remained independent but under the threat of Mexican invasion and reacquisition. There was strong sentiment for annexation in the Southern states because they believed that Texas would join the slave-holding section. The movement leading to annexation was inaugurated by President John Tyler in the autumn of 1843. On October 16, 1843, the American secretary of state informed Texas that the United States was willing to reopen negotiations for the annexation of Texas. A treaty providing for annexation of Texas was submitted to the Senate on April 22, 1844. After debate forces opposed to annexation rejected the treaty on June 8, 1844. Simms composed the play in November, 1843, and wanted it produced at the exact time that the Senate debate was occurring over the annexation of Texas.

Simms was a longtime supporter of Texas annexation. He spoke for it in his campaign for the state legislature.[61] From 1844 to 1846, he served in the South Carolina House of Representatives, where he advocated unity of the South for its peculiar interests and expansion of slave-holding states westward. The longest political harangue in his novels is for Southern expansion to Texas and Mexico. This is made by the character Kingsley in *Confession* (first published, 1841).[62] In 1844 Simms served on a committee in Barnwell District for the annexation of Texas; he asked that Southerners withhold their vote for any presidential candidate opposed to annexation.[63]

In early 1845 before annexation had taken place, Simms wrote to Armistead Burt, South Carolina Congressman, about Texas and the purpose of his play *Michael Bonham.* He said that he had taken no part in electing Polk president except "to stump it once or twice in favor of Texas." He added that he had done some pro-Texas writings, among which "a very Texan drama," unpublished in his desk, would make "a rumpus, be sure, if ever it reaches light upon the stage." He continued that he was "a genuine Southron," well hated by New England and hostile to Abolition.[64] By "Southron" Simms meant a loyal Southerner, who fiercely defended the political position of the South. It is, thus, signficant that he published *Michael Bonham* in both the *Southern Literary Messenger* and in the separate volume as "By a Southron," thereby emphasizing the political nature of the drama.

Simms saw the opposition to Texas as based on the slavery issue. In a letter to James Lawson, November 27, 1844, he enclosed a copy of a speech by his friend James H. Hammond, then governor of South Carolina, with whom he was in agreement. Hammond stated that the obstruction to annexation of Texas was owing to the deadly animosity of a portion of the Union to domestic slavery.

Two topical allusions to the Congressional debates on slavery and Texas emphasize the political nature of this play. In Part I, Scene 1, Michael Bonham has reprimanded Davy Crockett for talking too much. Crockett answers that if he were "Quincy Adams now, you would lecture me in vain. He, poor fellow, can't help his tongue." This remark is an allusion to John Quincy Adams' continued speaking against slavery and his opposition to the annexation of Texas as a slave-holding state at the time Simms was writing.

In Part V, Scene 9, Davy Crockett asks "Alabama" Davis if he has any news from the States, or Congress. Davis replies, "D——— Congress." He says it is made up of "old men's souls and old women's tongues." This is an allusion to Congressional debates on slavery and inaction on Texas annexation.

When *Michael Bonham* was presented on March 26, 27, 28,

1855, at the Charleston Theatre, the controversy over slavery had become heated. On May 30, 1854, the Kansas-Nebraska Act had passed. Afterwards Northern and Southern extremists rushed into Kansas to win it by ballots or bullets. Out of the debate on Kansas came the caning of Senator Charles Sumner by the South Carolina Congressman Preston S. Brooks on May 22, 1856. In this time of heightened sectional conflict, *Michael Bonham,* with the addition of the "Ode to Calhoun" at the end, served a new purpose. This was the glorification of Calhoun. The play that had advocated annexation of Texas was a fitting tribute to Calhoun. Calhoun had been a leader in the annexation of Texas. He accepted the position of secretary of state to accomplish it. He opposed England's purpose of making Texas independent and subservient to her commercial interests and a nursery for abolitionism.

Michael Bonham was hailed back at a time when Simms was idolizing the dead Calhoun and calling for a leader to equal him as a spokesman for the South and a defender of her interests. After Calhoun's death in 1850, Simms tried to spread his fame throughout the South.[66] He helped his important political acquaintance James H. Hammond compose a eulogy on Calhoun. On December 23, 1854, a few months before production of the play, Simms castigated Thomas Hart Benton and other politicians for their unfair view of Calhoun's career in a review of Benton's *Thirty Years' View* for the Charleston *Mercury.* He called for publication of Calhoun's works and a biography to give the South a guide for united effort.[67]

In his "Ode to Calhoun," Simms saw Calhoun as a heroic model. Simms said that Calhoun defended states' rights, but now the men in the Senate are incapable. Calhoun smote the reptile around our altar, "expelled the foe that threatened as a fate,/ And saved from loss the sacred shield of State!" Calling for a new leader, he said that if we raise an altar to him, "We may recall the genius, lost too soon,/ And find, 'mong other Sons, a new Calhoun."[68] Perhaps Simms is linking those fallen at the Alamo with Calhoun when he describes him as one who died in the midst of battle. "He died in harness, in the thick of strife,/ His very death a triumph—like his life!"[69]

Norman Maurice; or, The Man of the People

Simms wrote his best play, *Norman Maurice; or, The Man of the People*, in 1847. Its political purpose is to advocate admission of slave states from the West. It has another aim also. In *Norman Maurice*, Simms presents his concept of the good political leader. He portrays his qualities of courage against tyranny and his ability to follow his own counsel. The work is also interesting for the colloquial dialogue of its contemporary characters in blank verse. Simms thus tries to do what Maxwell Anderson attempted later in such a play as *Winterset* when he attempted to combine natural speech and poetry.

This play also illustrates well Simms's relationship with the theatre in Charleston and elsewhere. He wrote this play with Edwin Forrest in mind as the hero, but the actor was not interested. Next Simms tried to get a manager of the Charleston Theatre to produce the piece. Finally he negotiated with an actor in Nashville to perfrom it in St. Louis, but without success.

Simms composed *Norman Maurice* during a brief period in 1847. On July 31, 1847, he wrote James Lawson that he hoped to sit down soon to his tragedy.[70] On September 5, 1847, he wrote Lawson that he had sent Forrest one act of the play.[71] On September 23, 1847, he told Lawson that he had finished the play and liked it "as I wrote." He created the hero's role with Forrest in mind. His notion was that the audience would "identify him with it mentally & politically."[72] On October 26, 1847, Simms wrote Lawson that he was sure the story was "fresh & truly national." The hero was drawn very much "as an ideal," which he fancied Forrest would "gladly realize."[73] Simms certainly attempted to please Forrest. *Norman Maurice* has the same theme of freedom's triumph over tyranny as the most successful plays in which Forrest acted: *Metamora* (1829) by John Augustus Stone, *The Gladiator* (1831) by R. M. Bird, and *Jack Cade* (1835) by R. T. Conrad.

Simms held a high opinion of this play as is shown in his defense of its characters in a letter to Lawson in November, 1847.[74] In this letter, Simms's thoughts turned also to publication. He wrote that if *Norman Maurice* were not taken he would put all his plays in one volume and close his account with the "Dramatic World."[75] The play in fact appeared in six editions and in this way found a substantial audience. It was first published in 1851 as "Norman Maurice; or, The Man of the People. An American Drama," in the *Southern Literary Messenger,* 17 (April-August, 1851). Second, it appeared in the fall of 1851, as a pamphlet, published by John R. Thompson of Richmond, who also published *Michael Bonham.* Third, it was published in the *Southern Literary Gazette Supplement,* edited by Paul Hamilton Hayne, from June 19, 1852, No. 12 to July 31, 1852, No. 15. Fourth, it was published as *Norman Maurice,* "Fourth Edition, revised and corrected," by Lippincott, Grambo, and Cox, 1853, in Philadelphia. This edition was dedicated to Henry Gourdin "of South-Carolina," and also contained the following dramatic fragments in verse: "Caius Marius; An Historical Legend"; "Bertram; An Italian Sketch"; and "The Death of Cleopatra" (a dramatic dialogue of Augustus Caesar and Dolabella). Fifth, the play was published in 1853 in Simms's first volume of *Poems,* by John Russell, Charleston. Finally, the play was published in *Poems,* I, in 1853 as part of the Redfield edition. A comparison of the second edition (the pamphlet of 1851), before the revisions announced in the fourth edition, and the Redfield edition (the sixth edition and standard text) reveals only minor changes. For instance, in the last scene of the final act there is a slight change of wording at the beginning, and the opening lines of the speech of Clarice, Norman Maurice's wife, are added; but these revisions are minor.

After the publication of *Norman Maurice,* there were reviews in the magazines, mostly favorable. In 1851, Rufus W. Griswold praised the play but disliked the intrusion of politics, the meaning of which was quite plain to him. He said that the work presented the election of a senator from Missouri in the present time, as various passages disclosed. "This is one of the chief faults of the piece as the history of Missouri politics is so familiar that no illusion in the case is possible."[76] In 1852, the *Literary World* stated, "In Norman Maurice we have a noble ideal of many of the best qualities of our nature," such as trust and bravery.[77] In 1854, a reviewer for *Graham's* praised both the play and its political purpose in a review of "Simms's Works. New York: Redfield." He said that in Redfield's edition of Simms's Works, *Norman Maurice* in *Poems* was his favorite selection. The energy of style and "the direct reference of the plot and characterization to contemporary American politics, have given it a wider circulation than the other poems collected in these volumes."[78]

Simms's friends also spoke highly of the play. Thomas Holley Chivers, the Georgia poet, said that *Norman Maurice* was the best thing Simms had written and wondered why he did not concentrate on dramas.[79] The play was a favorite with James H. Hammond.[80] Paul Hamilton Hayne praised *Norman Maurice* in *Russell's Magazine*.[81]

Simms tried repeatedly to get *Norman Maurice* performed while it still had political relevance. On February 17, 1852, he wrote Francis Colburn Adams, a manager of the Charleston Theatre, about producing the play. He sent him a copy and suggested that Julia Dean, a popular actress at the Charleston Theatre, could do much with the part of Clarice if the theatre could find "a proper hero."[82] On February 24, 1852, Simms again wrote Adams that Miss Dean should have good acting support if the theatre undertook the play.[83]

Failing at the Charleston Theatre, Simms attempted to arrange performance in St. Louis, certainly appropriate since the play is set there. According to William P. Trent, an aspiring actor, George K.

Dickinson, rehearsed *Norman Maurice* in Nashville in 1854 and wrote Simms an exuberant letter about the triumph to be expected in St. Louis. Although Dickinson filled a St. Louis engagement, Christmas, 1854, and the *Missouri Republican* contained a glowing notice of Simms's new American play, shortly to be presented at the People's Theatre, the performance did not occur and Dickinson's letters suddenly ceased.[84]

Norman Maurice presents the title character's experiences in politics and his conflicts with the villainous Robert Warren, who tries to steal his wife. Maurice is a young lawyer in Philadelphia who finds recognition in an old, established society difficult. He wants to marry Clarice and does so over the objections of her malicious aunt, Mrs. Jervas, before going west. In St. Louis, the couple finds a happy life until Warren arrives in disguise. This man possesses a document with a forged signature by Maurice; Warren's document is a fraud, however, since he tricked Maurice into forging a name. The accusation against Maurice is to be confirmed by Richard Osborne, who is controlled by the tyrannical Warren, because Osborne acted as an accomplice in getting money from the forgery. Warren threatens to ruin Maurice's reputation and Maurice expels him from his house.

Next, Maurice is approached by Colonels Mercer and Brooks who want him to run for the Senate in Missouri. Maurice makes one stipulation: he will accept the election, but will not actively campaign as a candidate. They accept this condition. Mercer and Brooks then warn him against representing the Widow Pressley in court against an oppressor of the poor, Colonel Blasinghame, who is trying to seize her land. Maurice tells them he will proceed with the case. In the opposing political camp, Warren, introduced by his friend Harry Matthews, meets with Colonel Blasinghame and Colonel Ben Ferguson. The latter is to be the candidate of the opposing party. Ferguson agrees to let Warren accuse Maurice of forgery before the election.

Warren then visits Clarice in order to blackmail her; he says he will ruin Maurice in politics with this fatal secret unless Clarice consents to be his mistress. Clarice is horrified but agrees to give him her answer at sunset, when Warren will bring the incriminating document. Maurice, meanwhile, argues his case for the Widow Pressley and wins; he is challenged to a duel by Blasinghame and agrees to engage him with the small sword. Maurice disarms Blasinghame in the duel, but does not kill him and thereby leaves him a crushed man. At sunset Clarice stabs Warren after he gives her the document and attempts to embrace her.

Maurice now goes to the public caucus and gives his speech in support of the Constitution and its strict interpretation, the only safeguard of the Union, which is threatened with disintegration, he says. He is about to receive the vote of the caucus over Ferguson when the latter accuses him of a wrong in his past. Ferguson calls on Warren to provide the proof with his document containing the forgery. Matthews rushes in shouting that Maurice has murdered Warren. Maurice, however, proves from the testimony of witnesses that he could not have been present at the time and place where Warren was killed. Ferguson says Maurice has escaped the charge of murder but not forgery and calls on Osborne to confirm this crime. Osborne, now freed of Warren's tyrannical hold, declares that the charge is false and that Maurice is an honest, virtuous man. Ferguson and Matthews flee the meeting to the hisses of the crowd. After the vote of the public caucus in his favor, Maurice is elected by the legislative assembly.

In the last scene, we learn that Clarice has suffered a broken blood vessel and is dying. Maurice comes to her bedside and as he hears the cheers proclaiming him the next senator from Missouri, he wishes that the news could awaken his dead wife.

In summary, this highly melodramatic play presents Norman Maurice as the true man of the people in contrast to the false man, Ferguson, who is the tool of the people's oppressors. The triangle, involving Maurice, Clarice, and Warren, is connected with the political plot since Warren in his enmity wishes to destroy Maurice's marriage as well as his political career.

The good characters include Maurice, Clarice, the Widow Pressley, who represents the common people, and Colonels Mercer and Brooks, political leaders of the party supporting Maurice. The contrasting group consists of Ferguson, Blasinghame, Matthews, Warren, and Mrs. Jervas. Two characters who have been subject to tyrannical control, Osborne and Major Savage (the lackey of Blasinghame), break away from this evil influence.

The principal inspiration for *Norman Maurice* was the actor Edwin Forrest. The parallels between Forrest and the title character of this play illuminate the central theme of the ideal leader, who is the man of the people. Forrest, like Maurice, was from Philadelphia. He vociferously opposed tyranny. His championship of freedom over tyranny appears in the plays he made famous: *Metamora, The Gladiator,* and *Jack Cade.* Forrest also favored a strict interpretation of the Constitution and States' Rights.[85] Furthermore, Forrest was very much a man of the people in his political viewpoint. A member of the Democratic Party, he was aflame with Jacksonian democracy and belief in the common man.[86]

Forrest represented the common people in his famous dispute with the English actor William Charles Macready. He appealed to the masses with his animal vigor, as seen in *The Gladiator.* Macready was the favorite of the more refined audience. The conflict was in fact one between democracy and aristocracy. In the Astor Place Riot of 1849, Forrest's partisans attacked Macready's supporters as the "codfish aristocracy." Handbills were distributed saying that the time had come to decide if "English Aristocrats" would rule in the American metropolis or her own "Sons."[87]

Forrest's one venture into active politics reveals clear similarities with *Norman Maurice.* In 1838, Forrest was persuaded by the Democratic Party to make the July Fourth speech in New York. He spoke against tyranny. He declared that the Old World is cankered with the "longworn fetters of tyrannous habit," but "the empire of

the West" is in "the bloom and freshness of being."[88] The Demo-
crat-Republican Committee circulated the oration throughout the
country and asked him to become a political candidate. Forrest
however said he could not afford the loss of income.[89] In October,
1838, the New York nominating committee asked him to become a
candidate for the House of Representatives. On October 17, Forrest wrote them expressing his gratitude, but said he was "con-
strained to offer a negative reply."[90] He, like Maurice, was not to
be forced against his will into being a candidate. Forrest never delivered another political oration, but he maintained his passion for
political causes and contributed to the Democratic Party.[91]

Forrest's political excursion upset his fall acting engagement in
1838. Stephen Price, manager of the Park Theatre in New York,
observed Forrest's political dabbling, inferred that he intended to
quit the profession and so engaged foreign actors for the best part of
the season. Forrest was forced to go to the National Theatre. In
Philadelphia, Robert Maywood, manager of the Chestnut Street
Theatre, obeyed Price's dictates and Forrest was forced to the Walnut Street Theatre, then a secondary house. Forrest however succeeded at these theatres; the people rallied behind him.[92] This penalty incurred by Forrest for political activity would have discouraged him from performing in Simms's politically partisan play.

The political purpose of *Norman Maurice* was to support the ex-
tension of slavery west of Missouri into the territory won by the
Mexican War and to attack the well-known senator from Missouri,
Thomas Hart Benton. Since the play involves a Senate race in contemporary Missouri and Benton ran for the Senate in 1850 and
1854, the parallel would be clear to a contemporary reader, as
Rufus W. Griswold indicated in his review in 1851. The character who corresponds to Benton is appropriately Maurice's opponent,
Colonel Ben Ferguson, who is defeated. Allusions and similarities
between the character and Senator Benton make the parallel apparent. In the play, Matthews tells Warren that their candidate is
"Colonel Ben."[93] Benton was sometimes called "Col. Benton."[94]

Colonel Ben is said to have been one of the first lawyers to practice in Missouri (I.v). As early as 1815, Benton had come to Missouri, where he enjoyed a lucrative law practice.[95] At the public caucus, Mercer refers to Ferguson's "eloquence" and his "ancient reputation" (V.vi.). Benton's speeches were characterized by ornateness and pomposity, and he was in his fifth term of the Senate in 1847, when Simms wrote the play.

Certain facts concerning the slavery controversy and Benton demonstrate further that the play is dealing with this aspect of Benton's career. In 1820 Benton had opposed all slavery restriction in Missouri, but by 1828 he was in favor of gradual abolition. In 1847, notwithstanding instructions from the Missouri Legislature, he refused to uphold Calhoun's Resolutions of 1847 protecting slavery because he felt them subversive of the Union. Calhoun's Resolutions opposed the agitation on slavery recently evident in the attempt at the Wilmot Proviso, which would have prohibited slavery in the West. Calhun, demanding a strict interpretation of the Constitution, argued that enactment of any law regarding slavery in the new territories would be a violation of the Constitution, which said the people had a right to form their state governments as they chose.

Norman Maurice takes a similar stand to Calhoun. In his climactic speech, he trusts that in regard to the Constitution he speaks "the doctrine of Missouri." He would have it "a ligament of fix'd, unchanging value,/ Maintained by strict construction." It should not be "lopt" of its fair proportions by the ambitious demagogue, who with the baits of station in his eye will "sacrifice the State." Maurice continues that only the Constitution will prevent the worst peril that threatens to dissever the nation in the tempest:

> That married harmony of hope with power,
> Which keeps our starry Union o'er the storm,
> And in the sacred bond that links our fortunes,
> Makes us defy its thunders. (V.vi)

In the debates over Clay's Compromise of 1850, Benton opposed excessive concessions to the South. He was against the scheme of Calhoun's followers to draw the Missouri Compromise line through California. He thought the secessionists would only be satisfied with complete control of the goverment and thus considered the Compromise of 1850 a hollow sham. In 1851, his Missouri constituents defeated him in his sixth race for the Senate because of his opposition to slavery. From 1853-1855 he served in the House of Representative. In 1855, Benton was defeated for the Senate a second time, after claiming credit for the passage of the Kansas-Nebraska Act of 1854, which allowed new states to choose for themselves whether they would allow slavery.

Before and after the composition of *Norman Maurice* in 1847, Simms made critical comments on Senator Benton. He wrote Armistead Burt, South Carolina Congressman, on January 1, 1845, about Benton's opposition to slavery in the West. Simms thought his stand was "like him" but "scarcely so probable" of Missouri. He did not think Missourians were prepared for such a position.[96] After Benton failed to support Calhoun's Resolutions against slavery agitation in the spring of 1847, Simms wrote of his disapproval of the senator. On June 4, 1847, he wrote James H. Hammond that the Democratic Party, by its subservience to Senator Benton and others, had been doing its best to commit "felo de se."[97] In the Charleston *Mercury* of December 23, 1854, Simms reviewed Benton's *Thirty Years' View*. He castigated Benton for his unfair view of Calhoun's career.[98]

What makes this play exceptional is that it goes beyond a mere political purpose to deal with a provocative subject, the nature of the good political leader, one that has concerned thinkers from Plato to Machiavelli, from Shakespeare to Shaw. Because of this aspect, Simms was justified in his high estimate of the play.

First, the good political leader must possess courage. He must show bravery in the face of both external and internal enemies. Simms characterizes the true political leader as the foe of tyrants, his external enemies. Despite the dangers involved, Maurice defends the Widow Pressley against her oppressor, Colonel Blasinghame. He opposes Warren, who threatens him with a false charge and who is a tyrant over such men as Osborne. In Act V, Scene 6, he speaks also against such a "foreign despot" as Guizot or Palmerston.

In Act II, Scene 4, Maurice tells Clarice of his dream about a serpent's crushing her. The serpent's face resembled Warren's. He is disturbed, and Clarice tries to calm him. Warren in fact then does appear in St. Louis. He tells Maurice he possesses the secret that can ruin him and pulls out a pistol (II. vi). After ordering Warren away, Maurice in a soliloquy thinks about retiring from "the common market" and finding refuge in the wilderness. Then he realizes he is speaking "as if the serpent could not find the garden." It would be futile to flee from his enemies. He will not do so, but will face Warren and crush him at the "first show of evil." After this speech Maurice accepts the offer to become senator. When Clarice tells him that care should be gone now, he says that it will still come, but "the courage born of virtue / Hath still a holy sanction for its hope" (III.iii). Thus, despite fears, the desire to withdraw, and the certainty of anxiety, his internal enemies, the good political leader goes courageously forward with hope.

The comparison of Warren to the serpent is part of a pattern of imagery that emphasizes the threat that Maurice must face courageously. Warren is a devil figure and thus like his prototype a fearful destroyer. Warren is seen as the serpent who comes into the Eden of Maurice's marriage to destroy it. In Act I, Scene 4, Maurice in Philadelphia charges Warren with trying to steal Clarice's affections after he has shown him her picture. Maurice tells him he had not dreamed that he had admitted to his "Eden" the "serpent." Warren denies the charge, but when Clarice enters, he shows his guilt by fleeing. Maurice says, "Thus fled the fiend, touch'd by Ithuriel's spear" as he departed from "Eden." Warren is repeatedly referred to in devil imagery and called a reptile or serpent in the play. This serpent imagery stresses his treachery and desire to destroy, which Maurice must courageously oppose as he pursues his various activities as husband and future political leader.

The Edenic imagery points out the similarity of this play to the novels that Simms wrote about the Kentucky Tragedy. He published *Beauchampe* in 1842 and then divided the story into two novels, *Charlemont* (1856) and *Beauchampe* (1856) in the Redfield Edition. In presenting Colonel Sharpe as the serpent who comes to Margaret Cooper's Edenic village in Kentucky and later attempts to destroy the marriage of Margaret and Beauchampe, Simms uses much Edenic imagery.[99] Simm's version of the Beauchampe story has other parallels with *Norman Maurice*, which confirm a close relationship between these works: the triangle of husband, wife, and seducer; politics; and the Western setting.

The second quality that Simms names in the good leader is the most distinctive. The ideal political leader must be a good counselor. He should be able to follow his own counsel and to give and receive wise counsel. The subject of counsel occupied Simms many times in his writing, and it is one of the most interesting ideas with which he deals. The good counselor is seen in such a character as the scout Thumbscrew in *Mellichampe*, who persuades young Ernest Mellichampe to replace revenge with justice and fair play. Simms also has many bad counselors in his novels such as Guy Rivers in the novel of that name and M'Kewn in *Woodcraft*. Further, he published a whole volume of his own counsel called *Egeria* (1853), a collection of maxims. He explains in the introduction to this volume that Egeria was the Muse of Counsel, who advised Numa Pompilius, the Roman leader. In his last romance of the Revolution, *Joscelyn* (1867), Simms again presents a good political leader as he does in *Norman Maurice*. Stephen Joscelyn, like Norman Maurice, can give and receive good counsel and follow his own independent advice when necessary.[100]

In the portrayal of Maurice, the ability to keep his own counsel stands out. In Act II, Scene 1, Mercer and Brooks come to "counsel" with Maurice for the first time. Maurice listens to their warnings of the danger from Blasinghame. He replies that he will hold no "parley" with that "week day prudence" which teaches how much a virtue costs. He shows the men his letter to Blasinghame stating that he will prosecute the case of the Widow Pressley vs. Blasinghame to its conclusion without regard to consequences. Strengthened by Maurice's determination, Mercer and Brooks promise they will stand by him to the last.

The most important manifestation of Maurice's independent counsel comes in Act III, Scene 3, when Mercer and Brooks ask him to be their candidate for Senator. Maurice gives his conditions. He will not be "the creature of a selfish party" nor use "wealth or fraud" to rise to power. If the people, then, knowing these are his principles, "demand" his abilities, he will yield to their summons. This response to the people, however, "implies not/ One effort of my own. You, sirs, may make me/A Senator, but not a Candidate." Mercer and Brooks agree to these requirements, but ask him if he will speak at a meeting to enlighten the public on the issues. Maurice says that he will speak as he has always done when "a novel principle" demanded discussion. Maurice's refusal to campaign for votes as a candidate indicates that Simms's ideal politician is no Jacksonian Democrat who mixes gladly with the common people in a campaign. He is more in the mould of George Washington, who never campaigned for the presidency and refused a third term.

The statement "You, sirs, may make me a Senator, but not a Candidate" was a favorite with Simms and expresses his dislike of campaigning. On January 7, 1846, Simms wrote to Lawson about his labors in the state legislature, which he called "equally continuous & irksome." He reported that some of his constituents wanted him to run again. Simms said his answer was "you may elect me, but I will not electioneer."[101] Unlike Maurice, Simms was not elected.

James H. Hammond was surely another model for Norman

Maurice since in his political career he repeatedly refused to engage in campaigning, for instance, in the senatorial contest of 1846.[102] Later, on January 10, 1859, Simms wrote Hammond, then senator from South Carolina, in regard to the latter's becoming a presidential candidate of the Democratic Party. Such an office is not to be declined, he said, but remember "what Norman Maurice says—You may make me, Sirs,/A Senator, but not a Candidate." He advised Hammond to do nothing himself "directly or indirectly, either to promote or prevent" his election. That is, he should not be an active candidate for the presidency, but should accept the office if elected.

In addition to following his own counsel, Maurice will accept good counsel when given to him. In Act IV, Scene 2, Catesby tells Maurice that it was Savage who "advised" Maurice to be watchful of Blasinghame's doing him violence. Maurice listens carefully to this report and says he thanks Savage for this advice. Maurice can also give counsel, as his enemies recognize. Matthews tells Warren that Maurice "guides the councils" of his party and with such prudent skill that they "fancy" he is only their "mouth-piece." In fact, Maurice gives "the breath of life to them" (II.v).

As the opposing candidate, Ferguson makes an illuminating contrast because he points up the nature of the bad political leader. Ferguson is a pawn of Blasinghame because he is his lawyer in the case against the poor Widow Pressley. He is not the man of the people but rather the creature of the wealthy tyrant and the revengeful man. He succumbs to their bad counsel and thus lacks the indispensable quality of a political leader, the ability to follow his own counsel.

Ferguson's failure to take his own counsel comes out graphically in his acceptance of Warren's nefarious scheme to ruin Maurice by presenting the charge of forgery. In Act III, Scene 1, Warren departs for a "secret council" with Ferguson. At this meeting, in the next scene, Blasinghame announces peremptorily that Ferguson is to be the candidate for the Senate. Ferguson asks why not Blasinghame. The latter says his case against Widow Pressley needs "careful nursing now" and he cannot spare the time. Ferguson's meek acceptance of candidacy sharply contrasts with the conditions that Maurice lays down.

When Warren introduces his plan at the council, Matthews and Blasinghame approve it without even knowing what his secret is. Ferguson also accepts the scheme against Maurice, "though I much prefer that we should beat him,/In a fair wrestle, with the usual agents" (III.ii). Again, in Act IV, Scene 2, Ferguson cannot follow his own independent principles. After Warren has told Ferguson alone of the secret of the fraudulent document, he says "I do not like this business but our need/Will not permit that we discuss its merits." He weakly accepts a strategy which is against his moral scruples. He has followed therefore the unwise counsel of others, not his own best judgment.

It should be noted that those who follow bad counsel fall, whereas those who repudiate it rise. Matthews, who was lured into the plot by Warren, is proved a liar and hissed away by the crowd. On the contrary, Osborne opposes Warren's control and in the end refuses to make a false charge against Maurice. He does not meet Matthews' fate. Major Savage rejects the influence of Blasinghame. In Act V, Scene 3, when Savage sees Maurice spare Blasinghame's life after disarming him, he says, you're "a man/Among ten thousand, Maurice." In Act V, Scene 5, Ferguson says that Savage grows more friendly to Maurice than to him. Thus Savage changes from serving Blasinghame and Ferguson to admiring Maurice.

It is fitting to conclude this study of plays for the Charleston theatre with *Norman Maurice* because it is the best play of the most skilled and important writer to compose for the Charleston stage, William Gilmore Simms. This play effectively combines political purpose and serious treatment of an important subject.

VI

CONCLUSIONS: CHARLESTON DRAMATISTS AND AMERICAN DRAMA

*I*n estimating the part played by the Charleston dramatists in the development of American drama, a comparison should be made first with dramatists in other Southern cities. In the South before the Civil War, the Charleston theatre led in original dramatic writing for the stage because of the large quantity of original plays produced and published and because of the length of time they covered, from the 1790's to the Civil War.

Dramatic writing in Charleston can best be compared with that for theatres in Virginia and New Orleans. Dramatists in Virginia started composing earlier than in Charleston, but the lack of any strong single theatre equal to Charleston's meant that the writing in that state was intermittent and often ended as closet drama because of the difficulty of getting the play performed. We find a play here and there presented for the first time in Richmond, Petersburg, Norfolk, or Fredericksburg, but these works do not form a cohesive body of writing. The most active theatre was in Richmond.

An interesting play for the Richmond stage shows the tendency apparent in Charleston to deal with state topics. Albert Gilliam of Richmond wrote the second play on the Pocahontas theme; the first was James N. Barker's *The Indian Princess. or The First Settlement of Virginia* (1808). Gilliam's play is *Virginia, or Love and Bravery*, first acted at the Richmond Theatre, May 27, 1829, but not published. Characters include Captain John Smith, King Powhatan, and Pocahontas.[1] Other plays of Virginia show the uneven nature of writing in that state: Robert Munford wrote *The Candidates* and *The Patriots* (pre-Revolutionary pieces illustrating Virginia life); they were published in 1798, but there is no record of performance. Three closet dramas by well-known Virginians were *Almoran and Hamet* (1798), a play with an Eastern setting by William Munford; *The Wheel of Fortune* (1798), an anti-British play by St. George Tucker; and *The Path of Pleasure* by William Wirt. John Daly Burk who settled in Petersburg, wrote *Bethlem Gabor* (1807) for the theatre there. Its setting is Hungary and it praises political revolution.[2]

The city that compares most interestingly with Charleston is New Orleans. It was similar to Charleston in the large quantity of plays written by local citizens and in refuting abolition plays. New Orleans, however, did not see any appreciable number of original plays in English until the 1820's; thus it lacks plays about the Revolution and the Federalist-Republican period found in Charleston. Furthermore, the number of plays that were published is much smaller than in Charleston and thus its writing does not exist comparably as literature that can be assessed today.

New Orleans was like Charleston in glorifying a nearby battle; C. E. Grice, a native of New Orleans, wrote *The Battle of New Orleans*. His drama was published in Baltimore by the Commercial Press in 1815. It was first performed at the Park Theatre, New York, July 4, 1816.[3] This play was not produced in New Orleans until 1824. Afterwards, however, it became a patriotic standby. It was given on Washington's birthday, 1828; on the anniversary of the battle, January 8, 1844 and January 8, 1845; and three times in 1861. It achieved a total of eight performances in New Orleans.[4]

New Orleans resembled Charleston in staging many plays of local and topical interest. From 1806 to 1865 over seven hundred local and topical plays were given in New Orleans.[5] All but a few are lost.[6] Many of these were by residents of the city. The records of theatres in New York, Boston, Philadelphia, and Charleston show also that these cities had large segments of their theatre schedules devoted to local and topical plays.[7] Notice the similarity of these plays of local interest: in New Orleans, "Did You Ever Send Your Wife to the Lake?"; in New York, J. S. Coyne, "Did You Ever Send Your Wife to Brooklyn?"; in Charleston, "Did You Ever Send Your Wife to Mount Pleasant?"[8]

New Orleans took the same opposition to anti-slavery plays as Charleston. An original satire on *Uncle Tom's Cabin* (*Uncle Tom's Cabin in Louisiana*, by Dr. William T. Leonard,) was performed on the New Orleans stage. It opened March 6, 1854, at Dan Rice's New Amphitheatre and had an almost unprecedented run of twenty-three performances.[9] Dion Boucicault's *The Octoroon* was not welcome in New Orleans, nor in Charleston. It was not performed in New Orleans until the Federal forces controlled the city, when it was seen on April 5, 6, 7, 1865. On December 24, 1859, the *Daily Picayune* reviewer, having seen it in the North, described the characters as "ridiculous."[10]

New Orleans differs from Charleston in that the original plays written for its stage increased from the 1840's to the Civil War, reflecting the increase of importance of that city and the decrease of Charleston. Many local pieces about New Orleans life appeared, such as T. B. Logan's *Romance of the City* (1854) and J. E. Durivage's *New Orleans As It Is* (1848).[11] The Mexican War produced many pieces for its stage. An example was *Buena Vista,* performed July 4, 1847, at the American Theatre. It was by "a gentleman of this city" and described General Zachary Taylor's victory at Buena Vista.[12] This play, like others about the Mexican War given in New Orleans, was not published.

A comparison of the Charleston theatre with Northern theatres brings out most obviously the differences, such as the greater volume of original plays composed for the main New York and Philadelphia theatres, the emergence of professional dramatists like William Dunlap, George Henry Boker, and Dion Boucicault, and the popularity of anti-slavery plays. Another significant difference should be pointed out. In the North, though dramatists often wrote for the theatre in their place of residence as in Charleston, there developed the practice of having plays produced at theatres elsewhere as well. Many of the first dramatists were residents of Philadelphia, but because of the nearness and growing importance of New York as the theatrical center, their plays were performed first in New York. James N. Barker composed *Marmion* for a Philadelphia manager, but the play was performed first in New York, April 3, 1812.[13] R. M. Bird and George H. Boker were in the Philadelphia group, but their plays were not always performed there first.[14] Bird's *Gladiator* was first performed at the Park Theatre, New York, September 26, 1831.[15] Boker's *Francesca da Rimini* was given first at the Broadway Theatre, September 26, 1855.[16] There also developed in the North the actor-dramatist, whose plays were composed for various theatres. John Howard Payne's plays were often performed first at the Park Theatre in New York.[17] Some, however, appeared first in England. Payne's *Charles II* (composed with Washington Irving) was premiered at Covent Garden on May 27, 1824, and his *Clari* was first performed in London.[18]

A similarity between theatres in the North and Charleston is the dramatization of battles in the local area. Examples are Burk's *Bunker Hill* (first performed at the Haymarket Theatre, Boston, February 17, 1797); Dunlap's *André* (whose setting is New York state), at the Park Theatre, 1798; *The Battle of Lake Champlain* by A. J. Allen (at the Green St. Theatre, Albany, 1815); and *The*

Battle of Germantown, by Walter Leman (at the Walnut St. Theatre, Philadelphia, April 10, 1845).[19]

As the nation entered the period of heated sectional controversy, anti-slavery plays became prominent in the North. Some plays however attempted to placate the South and some called for reconciliation. Northern theatres to this extent showed more opportunity for free exchange of ideas on the subject. *Uncle Tom's Cabin* and *Dred* by Harriet Beecher Stowe became popular abolitionist plays, but the former makes the villain a Yankee. Dion Boucicault's *The Octoroon* seems to accept some Southern arguments by depicting kindness to slaves and presents a young Southerner, George Peyton, as completely unprejudiced on race. Two plays given in New York on the eve of the war advocate a conciliatory attitude toward the South: *A Southerner Visits New York* (1859) and *The Real Uncle Tom* (1860).[20] At the Charleston Theatre, the Southern position found expression in a burlesque of *Uncle Tom's Cabin* (1853) and in the production of Simms's *Michael Bonham* (1855), which praised Texas annexation and in an ode after the play called for a leader to replace John C. Calhoun.

In assessing dramatic writing in Charleston with regard to the evolution of American drama, four conclusions can be drawn from this study. First, the original pieces written for the Charleston theatre serve as an accurate barometer of the major concerns which attracted public opinion significantly in the South and nation from 1790 to 1860. Although not all the major issues reached the stage, those that did reveal what was on the minds of the people. There is a noticeable trend from a national to a sectional outlook. From 1790 to 1810 the pro-French, pro-Republican plays represent a national political view. When we consider Simms's plays dealing with the western territories, however, it is clear that the slavery issue has arisen to make the viewpoint distinctly sectional. This shift agrees with the general political movement in the South from national to sectional.

Second, the original pieces written for the Charleston theatre from the earliest period on show a regional flavor. The Revolutionary pageants depicted battles around Charleston, like *Attack on Fort Moultrie.* Ioor's play in the first decade of the century dealt with the climactic battle of the Revolution in South Carolina, the Battle of Eutaw Springs. White's one play with a political purpose presented Jackson's victory at New Orleans and his invasion of Florida. In *Michael Bonham,* Simms dramatized the eve of the Battle of the Alamo, in Texas, which was considered a part of the South.

Third, the two most important plays to emerge from this study are *The Battle of Eutaw Springs* and *Norman Maurice.* The former is the first published play by a native South Carolinian. It contains characters that have become familiar in Simms's works and other Southern literature: the humorous old Southern gentleman; the vivacious, daring Southern belle; and the Revolutionary heroes, like the romantic Swamp Fox. The other play that stands out is Simms's *Norman Maurice.* This work presents an interesting concept of the ideal political leader. He can follow his own counsel and is courageous despite dangers that tempt him to withdraw from public life. This play compares well in interest for the modern reader with other American plays of the time.

Fourth, certain names stand out from this account of the Charleston theatre and its dramatists. Alexander Placide, who was active in Charleston from 1794 to 1812, launched the tradition of vital dramatic writing. Without him this account of Charleston plays would be much different. He wrote and acted in pantomimes that were pro-French during a time when that meant to take a political position in favor of decisive independence from Great Britain, and he sponsored strongly Republican plays like Ioor's *Independence.* He continued the support of the battle play *Bunker Hill* and presented *The Battle of Eutaw Springs*, thus aiding the development of this versatile dramatic form. He produced the largest number of original pieces of any manager at the Charleston theatre; seven of these were published. Placide epitomizes the pro-French, pro-Republican attitude of South Carolina, beginning in the 1790's.

William Ioor, a physician, felt so strongly about the drama and politics that he wrote and defended vigorously his two plays, the first about the small farmer and the second about the Battle of Eutaw Springs. He was a pioneer in writing for the theatre and in dramatizing and idealizing the Revolution in South Carolina. His enthusiasm for the drama and his political partisanship exemplify the vigorous spirit of men interested in the theatre during the Federalist-Republican period from 1790 to 1812.

John Blake White is most distinctive for his social concerns. Although the South was never as reform oriented as New England, in the first decades of the nineteenth century certain movements received much support. White accurately expressed the social conscience of the South in two plays. He attacked dueling and also the evil of alcoholism.

Finally there is Simms, the dominant figure in dramatic writing for the three decades before the Civil War. Simms serves as the representative dramatist for this time. It was he who used the stage to argue the South's position on the primary issue, slavery. In his two main plays, *Michael Bonham* and *Norman Maurice*, he did not directly defend slavery, but he favored the admission of states to the Union that would allow it. Simms was in the best tradition of the Charleston theatre since he valued it highly. He supported the theatre publicly, wrote theatrical criticism, offered plays for its stage, employed the theatre as a political platform, and served as the historian of its dramatists, when he wrote "Early Authors and Artists" for the *XIX Century*.

The dramatists of the Charleston theatre, from Ioor to Simms, present accurately Southern attitudes for their times. Because they give their own distinctive story, they are necessary to complete the national picture of American drama. Since these dramatists joined the increasing national tendency to present American material,

characters, and concerns during the period of romantic nationalism, they assisted importantly in the formation of American
drama.

APPENDIX

Principal Charleston Dramatists

	First Performance[1]	Publication Date	Number of Performances
James Workman (?-1832)			4 (1 in
Liberty in Louisiana	1804	1804	Savannah)[2]
William Ioor (1780-1850)			
Independence	1805	1805	3
The Battle of Eutaw Springs	1807	1807	6 (1 in Richmond, 1 in Philadelphia)
John Blake White (1781-1859)			
Foscari	1806	1806	4
The Mysteries of the Castle	1806	1807	3
Modern Honor	1812	1812	3
The Triumph of Liberty	—	1819	0
The Forgers	—	1837	0
Isaac Harby (1788-1828)			
The Gordian Knot	1810	1810	2
Alberti	1819	1819	2
William Crafts (1787-1826)			
The Sea-Serpent	1819	1819	3 (1 in Richmond)
James Wright Simmons (c. 1790-1858)			
Manfredi	—	1821	0
Valdemar	—	1822	0
Ravenswood	1824	—	2
De Montalt, or the Abbey of St. Clair	1843	—	1

Augustus Julian Requier
(1825-1887)

The Spanish Exile	1844	1844	2
Marco Bozzaris	—	1860	0

William Gilmore Simms
(1806-1870)

Michael Bonham; or,			
The Fall of Bexar	1855	1852	3
Norman Maurice; or,			
The Man of the People	—	1851	0

NOTES

Preface

1. I am particularly indebted to Arthur Hobson Quinn, *A History of the American Drama from the Beginning to the Civil War* (1923; second edition, New York: Appleton-Century-Crofts, 1943); Eola Willis, *The Charleston Stage in the XVIII Century* (Columbia: The State Co., 1924); and W. Stanley Hoole, *The Ante-bellum Charleston Theatre* (Tuscaloosa: Univ. of Alabama Press, 1946).

2. See, for example, Edd Winfield Parks, *Segments of Southern Thought* (Athens: Univ. of Georgia Press, 1938), pp. 140-141; and Hoole, p. xvi.

Chapter I

1. Glenn Hughes, *A History of the American Theatre, 1700-1950* (New York: Samuel French, 1951), p. 90. The Charleston "theatre" refers to all theatres taken together in the city. "The Charleston Theatre" will refer to a specific theatre.

2. Watson Nicholson, *Anthony Aston, Stroller and Adventurer* (South Haven, Michigan: published by the author, 1920), p. 59, cited by Julia Curtis, "The Early Charleston Stage; 1703-1798" (Diss., Indiana Univ., 1968), p. 1, hereafter referred to as Curtis, "Early Charleston Stage."

3. George O. Seilhamer, *History of the American Theatre* (3 volumes, Philadelphia: Globe Printing House, 1888-1891; reprint, New York: Greenwood Press, 1968), I, 331-332.

4. Hugh S. Rankin, *The Theater in Colonial America* (Chapel Hill: Univ. of North Carolina Press, 1965), pp. 25, 27. In commemoration of this first theatre, the building now occupied by the present dramatic company in Charleston is called the Dock Street Theatre.

5. *The Charleston Stage in the XVIII Century* (Columbia: The State Co., 1924), p. 59.

6. For information on West, see Susanne K. Sherman, "Thomas Wade West, Theatrical Impresario, 1790-1799," *The William and Mary Quarterly*, Third Series, 9 (Jan., 1952), 10-28.

7. Ibid., pp. 22-23.

8. Robert Mills, *Statistics of South Carolina* (Charleston, 1826), p. 423, cited by Julia Curtis, "The Architecture and Appearance of the

Charleston Theatre, 1793-1833," *Educational Theatre Journal,* 23 (1971), 10.

9. Curtis, ibid., pp. 10-11.

10. *State Gazette of South Carolina,* Dec. 17, 1793, cited by Curtis, "Early Charleston Stage," pp. 216-217.

11. Curtis, ibid., pp. 216-217.

12. Cited by Willis, p. 167.

13. George C. Rogers, Jr., *Charleston in the Age of the Pinckneys* (Norman: Univ. of Oklahoma Press, 1969), p. 110.

14. George C. Rogers, Jr., *A South Carolina Chronology 1497-1970* (Columbia: Univ. of South Carolina Press, 1973), p. 50.

15. *City Gazette and Daily Advertiser,* March 20, 1795, cited by Curtis, "Early Charleston Stage," p. 243; *City Gazette and Daily Advertiser,* April 10, 1794, cited by Curtis, "Early Charleston Stage," pp. 245-246.

16. Charles Fraser, *Reminiscences of Charleston* (Charleston: S. Russell, 1854), p. 44, cited by Curtis, "Early Charleston Stage," p. 246.

17. *City Gazette and Daily Advertiser,* July 1, 1794, cited by Curtis, "Early Charleston Stage," pp. 265-266.

18. *South Carolina State Gazette and Timothy and Mason's Daily Advertiser,* July 29, 1794, cited by Curtis, "Early Charleston Stage," p. 272.

19. Curtis, "Early Charleston Stage," pp. 270, 274-275; *Columbian Herald and Southern Star,* Oct. 3 and Nov. 14, 1794, cited by Curtis, "Early Charleston Stage," pp. 282, 286-287.

20. *Columbian Herald and Southern Star,* Feb. 11, 1795, cited by Curtis, "Early Charleston Stage," pp. 296-298; Curtis, "Early Charleston Stage," p. 454.

21. *South Carolina State Gazette and Timothy and Mason's Daily Advertiser,* April 30, 1795, cited by Curtis, "Early Charleston Stage," p. 309.

22. Willis, p. 361; Seilhamer, III, 360-362; William Dunlap, *History of the American Theatre* (1832; reprint, New York: Burt Franklin, 1963), I, 312-313, 371-372; Willis, pp. 377-378, 433, W. Stanley Hoole, *The Ante-bellum Charleston Theatre* (Tuscaloosa: Univ. of Alabama Press, 1946), pp. 66-74.

23. O. G. Brockett, "The European Career of Alexander Placide," *Southern Speech Journal,* 27 (Summer, 1962), 306-313; Curtis, "Early Charleston Stage," pp. 239, 240.

24. Hoole, p. 3.

25. Dunlap, II, 294.

26. "The Elder Placide, His Company and Contemporaries," *Spirit of the Times* (March 18, 1848), p. 44.

27. "Dr. Irving's Reminiscences of the Charleston Stage," ed. Emmett Robinson, *South Carolina Historical and Genealogical Magazine,* 52 (July, 1951), 168. This source is referred to hereafter as "Reminiscences." This journal will be abbreviated *SCHGM* and when the title changes to *South Carolina Historical Magazine, SCHM.*

28. Willis, p. 326.

29. "Reminiscences," *SCHGM*, 52 (July, 1951), 168. Matthew and Sara Sully came to Charleston in 1792 with a family of four sons and five daughters, a number of whom acted in the theatre. Their son, the well-known painter Thomas Sully, maintained his associations in Charleston for many years after leaving the city. See "Thomas Sully" in the *Dictionary of American Biography*.

30. Charleston *Times*, Jan. 13, 1807. Sully played the part of a comic character in this play.

31. Cited by Dunlap, I, 312-313.

32. Hoole, pp. 69-73, 78. Dates of all theatrical performances in Charleston after 1800 given in this volume have been checked in this source or in the Charleston *Courier* and hereafter will not be footnoted.

33. Cited in William Bullock Maxwell, *The Mysterious Father*, ed. Gerald Kahan (Athens: Univ. of Georgia Press, 1965), Appendix II, p. 56.

34. Sylvie Chevalley, "The Death of Alexander Placide," *SCHGM*, 58 (April, 1957), 63; Richmond *Enquirer*, Dec. 28, 1811.

35. "The Elder Placide," *Spirit of the Times* (March 18, 1848), p. 44.

36. "Reminiscences," *SCHGM*, 52 (April, 1951), 97.

37. Hoole, p. 15.

38. "Reminiscences," *SCHGM*, 53 (Jan., 1952), 40 and 52 (July, 1951), 170.

39. *Appleton's Cyclopaedia of American Biography* (New York: D. Appleton, 1887-89), II, 649.

40. "Reminiscences," *SCHGM*, 52 (Oct., 1951), 225.

41. Ibid., 52 (July, 1951), 177, 129. For William Gilmore Simms's impressions of Gilfert, see "The Humours of the Manager," in *Stories and Tales*, ed. John C. Guilds, *The Writings of William Gilmore Simms*, V (Columbia: Univ. of South Carolina Press, 1974).

42. Hoole, pp. 16-18.

43. Martin S. Shockley, "A History of the Theatre in Richmond, Virginia, 1819-1838," Diss. Univ. of North Carolina, 1938, p. 95.

44. The South Carolinian was Francis Kinloch Huger. He made the unsuccessful attempt after Lafayette was imprisoned in 1792. He accompanied Lafayette to South Carolina in 1825. See "Lafayette-Huger Letters," *SCHGM*, 60 (April, 1959), 57-65.

45. Hoole, p. 23.

46. "Reminiscences," *SCHGM*, 52 (July, 1951), 171.

47. Hoole, p. 21.

48. "Reminiscences," *SCHGM*, 52 (April, 1951), 97 and 51 (July, 1950), 129.

49. The following discussion of S. C. Carpenter is based on my article, "Stephen Cullen Carpenter: First Drama Critic of the Charleston *Courier*," *SCHM*, 69 (Oct., 1968), 243-252.

50. Willis, passim.

51. 'Reminiscences," *SCHGM,* 52 (April 1951), 99.

52. Quoted in William Charvat, *The Origins of American Critical Thought, 1810-1835* (Philadelphia: Univ. of Pennsylvania Press, 1936), p. 125.

53. Charvat, pp. 30-31, 131.

54. See Hoole, pp. 63-72.

55. William Ioor, *Independence* (Charleston: G. M. Bounetheau, 1805).

56. "Reminiscences," *SCHGM,* 52 (April, 1951), 99. For information on Holland, Harby, and Crafts, see chapter two. "Momford" is probably an error for E. Morford, associate editor of the *Courier* and founder of the *Mercury.* See William L. King, *The Newspaper Press of Charleston, S. C.* (Charleston: Edward Perry, 1872), p. 101. Jacob Newton Cardozo (1786-1876) was the editor of the *Southern Patriot* and the *Evening News;* he was an economist who championed free trade.

57. "Our Early Authors and Artists," *XIX Century,* 1 (Sept., 1869), 280.

58. Hoole, pp. 28-29, 31.

59. Tyrone Power, *Impressions of America During 1833-1836* (London, 1836), II, 93, cited by Hoole, p. 33.

60. Hoole, pp. 34-37.

61. Ibid., p. 38.

62. *Courier* (April 20, 1837), cited by Hoole, p. 39.

63. Hoole, p. 40.

64. "Reminscences," *SCHGM,* 51 (1950), 201.

65. Hoole, pp. 42, 44.

66. "Reminiscences," *SCHGM,* 51 (1950), 204; 52 (1951), 29.

67. Hoole, pp. 45-49.

68. Hoole, pp. 117-125. A dramatization of *The Yemassee* was given in New York on August 17, 1835. See *The Letters of William Gilmore Simms,* ed. Mary C. Simms Oliphant, et al., (Columbia: Univ. of South Carolina Press, 1953), II, 9, n.

69. *Letters of Simms,* (1952), I, 407; II, 214.

70. Hoole, pp. 133-153, 61, n.

71. Ibid., pp. 51-64.

72. The Rev. Thomas Smyth, *The Theatre, A School of Religion, Manners, & Morals* (Charleston: Jenkins and Hussey, 1838), pp. 13, 43.

73. *The Theatre Defended. A Reply to Two Discourses of the Rev. Thomas Smyth* (Charleston: Thomas J. Eccles, 1838), pp. 26, 30.

74. Louis Fitzgerald Tasistro, *Random Shots and Southern Breezes, Containing Critical Remarks on the Southern States and Institutions, with Semi-Serious Observations on Men and Manners* (New York: Harper and Brothers, 1842), II, 113-114, 129-131, cited by James H. Dormon, Jr., *Theatre in the Ante Bellum South* (Chapel Hill: Univ. of North Carolina

Press, 1967), pp. 136-137.
75. Dormon, p. 137.

Chapter II

1. John Beete, *The Man of the Times* (Charleston: W. P. Young, [1797]), Act. I, Scene 2.
2. Ibid.
3. Julia Curtis, "The Early Charleston Stage: 1703-1798" (Diss. Indiana Univ., 1968), pp. 403-404.
4. *Americana; or, a New Tale of the Genii* (Baltimore: W. Pechin, 1802).
5. Cited by Eola Willis, *The Charleston Stage in the Eighteenth Century* (Columbia, S. C.: The State Co., 1924), p. 383.
6. Ibid., p. 382.
7. The following discussion of the play is based on my article, "A Denunciation on the Stage of Spanish Rule: James Workman's *Liberty in Louisiana* (1804)," *Louisiana History*, 11 (Summer, 1970), 245-259.
8. Thomas P. Abernethy, *The Burr Conspiracy* (New York: Oxford Press, 1954), pp. 25, 168, 179-182, 227.
9. See Joseph Sabin, *Bibliotheca Americana* (New York, 1868-1938), XXIX, 107-109.
10. Arthur Hobson Quinn, *A History of the American Drama from the Beginning to the Civil War* (New York: Appleton-Century-Crofts, 1943), p. 135, n.; J. Max Patrick, *Savannah's Pioneer Theatre from Its Origins to 1810* (Athens: Univ. of Georgia Press, 1953), p. 68.
11. Abernethy, *Burr Conspiracy*, pp. 167-168; Garnie W. McGinty, *A History of Louisiana* (New York: Exposition Press, 1949), p. 106.
12. James Workman, *Liberty in Louisiana* (Charleston: Query and Evans, 1804), p. iv.
13. Thomas P. Abernethy, *The South in the New Nation, 1789-1819* (Baton Rouge: Louisiana State Univ. Press, 1961), pp. 255-256; Clarence E. Carter, ed., *Territorial Papers of the United States* (Washington: U. S. Government Printing Office, 1940), IX, 43, 45.
14. See Oliver Perry Chitwood and Frank Lawrence Owsley, *A Short History of the American People* (New York: D. Van Nostrand Co., 1945), I, 306, 318.
15. *The Female Enthusiast: A Tragedy in Five Acts* (Charleston: J. Hoff, 1807).
16. Much of the biographical information on Harby is taken from "A Memoir" by Abraham Moise in *A Selection from the Miscellaneous Writings of the late Isaac Harby*, ed. Henry L. Pinckney and Abraham Moise (Charleston: James S. Burges, 1829); and L. C. Moise, *Biography of Isaac Harby* (n. p., 1931).
17. William Gilmore Simms, "Our Early Authors and Artists," *XIX Century*, 1 (Sept., 1869), 280; L. C. Moise, pp. 21, 26.

18. L. C. Moise, p. 32.
19. Cited by L. C. Moise, p. 25, n.
20. Simms, "Our Early Authors," p. 280.
21. *A Selection from the Writings of Isaac Harby,* p. 14.
22. Ibid., p. 256.
23. Ibid., pp. 265-266.
24. William Charvat, *The Origins of American Critical Thought, 1810-1835* (Philadelphia: Univ. of Pennsylvania Press, 1936), p. 60.
25. *The Gordian Knot* (Charleston: G. M. Bounetheau, 1810), preface, p. v.
26. *Alberti* was published in 1829 in *A Selection from the Writings of Harby.*
27. Plays by Harby's predecessors at the Charleston Theatre: *The Mysteries of the Castle* (1806) by John Blake White and *The Battle of Eutaw Springs* (1807) by William Ioor.
28. *A Selection from the Writings of Harby,* p. 15.
29. *The Gordian Knot,* p. vi.
30. This play has been re-published in a modern edition. See William Bullock Maxwell, *The Mysterious Father,* ed. Gerald Kahan (Athens: Univ. of Georgia Press, 1965).
31. Patrick, pp. 79, 71.
32. Cited in Maxwell, Appendix II, p. 49.
33. Cited in ibid., pp. 52, 55-56.
34. Cited in ibid., pp. 49-50, 56.
35. The fact that this volume was reviewed by Washington Irving in the *Analetic Magazine* (1814) is an indication of the recognition that Holland's writing had already received. Irving's review has been reprinted in Clarence Arthur Brown, *The Achievement of American Criticism* (New York: Ronald Press, 1954).
36. Simms, "Our Early Authors and Artists," p. 281.
37. (Charleston: A. E. Miller, 1822). It is designated as "by a South-Carolinian."
38. Edwin C. Holland, *The Corsair* (Charleston: A. E. Miller, 1818), preface, p. vii.
39. William P. Trent, *William Gilmore Simms* (Boston: Houghton, Mifflin, 1892), pp. 26, 47.
40. This essay is included in William Crafts, *A Selection, in Prose and Poetry* (Charleston: Sebring and Burgess, 1828), pp. 321-322.
41. Herbert Ravenel Sass, *Outspoken, 150 Years of the News and Courier* (Columbia: Univ. of South Carolina Press, 1953), p. 22.
42. J. B. O'Neall, *Biographical Sketches of the Bench and Bar of South Carolina* (Charleston: Courtnay and Co., 1859), II, 361, 348.
43. V. L. Parrington, *Main Currents in American Thought* (New York: Harcourt, Brace, 1927-1930), II, 113.
44. Jay B. Hubbell, *The South in American Literature, 1607-1900*

(Durham, N. C.: Duke Univ. Press, 1954), p. 262.

45. William Crafts, *The Sea-Serpent* (Charleston: A. E. Miller, 1819).

46. O'Neall, II, 348.

47. Crafts, *A Selection*, p. 311.

48. Martin S. Shockley, "American Plays in the Richmond Theatre, 1819-1838," *Studies in Philology*, 37 (1940), 119.

49. "Our Early Authors and Artists," p. 282. For information on Crafts, see Vernon L. Parrington, *Main Currents in American Thought* II, 112-114; and J. B. Hubbell, *The South in American Literature, 1607-1900*, pp. 259-263.

50. *Manfredi* (Philadelphia: Moses Thomas, 1821) and *Valdemar* (Philadelphia: H. C. Carey and I. Lea, 1822).

51. *The Letters of William Gilmore Simms*, ed. Mary C. Simms Oliphant, Alfred Taylor Odell, and T. C. Duncan Eaves (Columbia: Univ. of South Carolina Press, 1952-1956), I, cxxxvii.

52. (Charleston: Archibald E. Miller, 1818.) For information on Miss Pinckney, see *The Library of Southern Literature*, ed. Edwin Anderson Alderman, *et al.* (New Orleans: Martin and Hoyt, 1908-1913), XV, 345.

53. (1854, reprint, New York: W. W. Norton, 1961), p. 509. This novel was called *The Sword and the Distaff* when first published in 1852.

54. "The Drama of South Carolina," *Southern Literary Gazette* (Aug. 15, 1829), p. 153.

55. *Letters of Simms*, III, 162-163.

56. *Magnolia, or Southern Apalachian*, 2 (March, 1843), 208.

57. James H. Dormon, Jr. *Theatre in the Ante Bellum South* (Chapel Hill: Univ. of North Carolina Press, 1967), pp. 130-131.

58. Quinn, p. 284.

59. Ibid., p. 288.

60. Ibid., pp. 289, 290.

61. Dormon, 278; *Courier*, Oct. 24, 1853, cited by Dormon, p. 279.

62. *Dictionary of American Biography, sub nomine*. I have found no extant copy of this play.

63. *The Old Sanctuary* is listed in Joseph Sabin's *Bibliotheca Americana; Poems* is listed in James Gibson Johnson, *Southern Fiction Prior to 1860: An Attempt at a First-Hand Bibliography* (Charlottesville, Virginia: Mitchie Co., 1909), p. 74.

Chapter III

1. See Jay B. Hubbell's chapter on Munford in *The South in American Literature* (Durham: Duke Univ. Press, 1954), p. 142-148; and Rodney M. Baine, *Robert Munford: America's First Comic Dramatist* (Athens: Univ. of Georgia Press, 1967).

2. Dorchester was twenty-six miles from Charleston on the north bank of the Ashley River. The biographical information on Ioor has been ob-

tained principally from the *Dictionary of American Biography,* his obituary in the *Courier* (August 10, 1850), and a collection of family records provided by Miss Elizabeth McDavid of Pelzer, South Carolina, a descendant of Dr. Ioor.

3. Harriot Horry Ravenel, *Charleston: The Place and the People* (New York: Macmillan, 1906), pp. 23-24, 253.

4. Joseph Ioor Waring, *A History of Medicine in South Carolina, 1670-1825* (Columbia: South Carolina Medical Association, 1964), pp. viii, 383.

5. William Ioor, *Independence* (Charleston: G. M. Bounetheau, 1805).

6. Walter B. Edgar, ed. *Biographical Directory of the South Carolina House of Representatives, Session Lists 1692-1973* (Columbia: Univ. of South Carolina, 1974), I, 256, 261.

7. William Ioor, *The Battle of Eutaw Springs* (Charleston: J. Hoff, 1807).

8. Matthew Sully, a popular member of the company, played the part of Queerfish, a comic character in the play.

9. Richmond *Enquirer,* September 27, 1811.

10. Reese D. James, *Old Drury of Philadelphia* (Philadelphia: Univ. of Pennsylvania Press, 1932), p. 21; Arthur Hobson Quinn, *A History of the American Drama from the Beginning to the Civil War* (New York: Appleton-Century-Crofts, 1943), p. 155.

11. Rosser H. Taylor, *Ante-Bellum South Carolina: A Social and Cultural History* (Chapel Hill: Univ. of North Carolina Press, 1942), p. 43.

12. Waring, p. 383.

13. "Our Early Authors and Artists," *XIX Century,* 1 (Sept., 1869), 279-280.

14. Information from Professor Raven Ioor McDavid, Jr., a descendant of Ioor.

15. Hazel Crowson Sellers, *Old South Carolina Churches* (Columbia: Crowson Printing Co., 1941), after plate 55.

16. The following discussion of this play is based on my article, "Jeffersonian Republicanism in William Ioor's *Independence,* the First Play of South Carolina," *South Carolina Historical Magazine,* 69 (July, 1968), 194-203.

17. Quinn, p. 188; and Ludwig Lewisohn, "Books We Have Made, A History of Literature in South Carolina," Part III, Charleston *News and Courier,* Sunday News, July 5—September 20, 1903.

18. See Wilfred E. Binkley, *American Political Parties* (New York: Knopf, 1962), p. 78, for a statement on the unifying effect of this belief.

19. *The Independent. A Novel,* 2 vols. (London: T. Cadell, 1784).

20. *British Museum General Catalogue of Printed Books,* Vol. 111.

21. Additions and significant alterations to the novel by Ioor will be clearly indicated in this analysis. If not so indicated, passages from the

play have exact, or close, equivalents in the novel.

22. Thomas Jefferson, *Notes on the State of Virginia*, ed. William Peden (Chapel Hill: Univ. of North Carolina Press, 1955), p. 175.

23. David Ramsay, *The History of South-Carolina, from its first settlement in 1670 to the year 1808* (Charleston: David Longworth, 1809), II, 413-414.

24. John Drayton, *A View of South-Carolina, as respects her natural and civil concerns* (Charleston: W. P. Young, 1802), p. 221.

25. Jefferson, p. 165.

26. Ibid.

27. Ramsay, II, 414.

28. Lewis Cecil Gray, *A History of Agriculture in the Southern United States to 1860* (Washington: Carnegie Institute of Washington), I, 451, 488, 490.

29. Charles A. Beard, *Economic Origins of Jeffersonian Democracy* (New York: Macmillan, 1915), p. 423.

30. Cited by Gray, I, 499.

31. Lewisohn, "Books We Have Made," Part III.

32. See Binkley, p. 76, for a comment on Republican dislike of lawyers.

33. *A History of the American Bar* (Boston: Little, Brown, 1911), pp. 212-214.

34. David Duncan Wallace, *South Carolina: A Short History, 1520-1948* (Chapel Hill: Univ. of North Carolina Press, 1951), pp. 410-411.

35. Ramsay, II, 159.

36. Ibid., pp. 413-414.

37. Binkley, pp. 72-73.

38. Wallace, p. 362.

39. See Ramsay, II, 395.

40. Drayton, p. 221.

41. Ravenel, pp. 384-386.

42. George C. Rogers, Jr., *Charleston in the Age of the Pinckneys* (Norman: Univ. of Oklahoma Press, 1969), pp. 150-151.

43. William Ioor, *The Battle of Eutaw Springs* (Charleston: J. Hoff, 1807).

44. John Harold Wolfe, *Jeffersonian Democracy in South Carolina* (Chapel Hill: Univ. of North Carolina Press, 1940), pp. 206-207, 210.

45. Samuel Flagg Bemis, *A Diplomatic History of the United States* (New York: Holt, Rinehart and Winston, 1965), pp. 144-145.

46. Theodore Thayer, *Nathanael Greene* (New York: Twayne, 1960), pp. 399, 409.

47. For Simms's treatment of this subject, see C. Hugh Holman, "William Gilmore Simms's Picture or the Revolution as a Civil Conflict," *Journal of Southern History*, 15 (Nov., 1949), 441-462.

48. Thayer, p. 368.

49. Wolfe, p. 198.

50. Russell Nye observes that characters first appeared in early plays that later become famous in American drama, poetry, and fiction; he cites as examples Pocahontas, the raw frontiersman, and the Revolutionary soldier-hero. *The Cultural Life of the New Nation, 1776-1830* (New York: Harper and Row, 1960), p. 266.

51. Simms, "Our Early Authors and Artists," 279-280.

52. *Eutaw* (1856; rpt., New York: A. C. Armstrong, 1882), pp. 67-68.

53. Simms, *The Life of Francis Marion* (New York: G. F. Cooledge, 1844), p. vi.

54. *The Battle of Eutaw Springs*, Act IV, Scene 2 and Act V, Scene 2; David Ramsay, *The History of the Revolution of South-Carolina from a British Province to an Independent State* (Trenton: Isaac Collins, 1785), II, 254; William Moultrie, *Memoirs of the American Revolution* (New York, 1802, reprinted by the *New York Times* and Arno Press, 1968), II, 295, 357-358.

55. John Chester Miller, *Triumph of Freedom* (Boston: Little, Brown, 1948), p. 597; Thayer, pp. 380, 377.

56. It is only fair to say in Ioor's behalf that among the numerous writings on this battle, from the first to the most recent, there are frequent variations both in facts and appraisals.

57. Moultrie, I, 292-293. The incident is not mentioned by Ramsay.

58. This information is derived from Edward McCrady, *The History of South Carolina in the Revolution, 1780-1783* (New York: Macmillan, 1902), p. 447; Robert D. Bass, *Swamp Fox: The Life and Campaigns of General Francis Marion* (New York: Henry Holt, 1959), p. 216; Thayer, pp. 375-376; Simms, *Eutaw*, pp. 513-514.

59. Moultrie, II, 294; Thayer, p. 378; Bass, p. 218.

60. McCrady, p. 460; David Duncan Wallace, *The History of South Carolina* (New York: American Historical Society, 1934), II, 289-290; Thayer, pp. 379-380.

61. Simms, *The Life of Nathanael Green* (New York: Darby and Jackson, [1849]), p. 339; P. Horry and M. L. Weems, *The Life of General Francis Marion* (Philadelphia: J. P. Lippincott, 1860), p. 234.

62. Simms, *Eutaw*, pp. 521, 531; McCrady, pp. 455-456; Bass, p. 218; Thayer, p. 378.

63. See the following chapter and W. P. Trent, *William Gilmore Simms* (Boston: Houghton Mifflin, 1892), pp. 8-9.

64. This information on Ioor's first letter has been obtained from references in the *Courier*, July 8, 1806. No copy of the July 2, issue of the *City Gazette* has been found. Ioor evidently chose this pseudonym because his name was sometimes written "William Joor," and he was a young man.

65. Ioor is referring to the comic soldier, Queerfish.

66. See the discussion of Carpenter above, chapter one.

67. Simms, "Our Early Authors and Artists," 279-280.

68. Arthur Hobson Quinn, *A History of the American Drama from the Beginning to the Civil War* (New York: Appleton-Century-Crofts, 1943), p. 155.

69. See Montrose J. Moses, *The American Dramatist* (Boston: Little, Brown, 1925), p. 92; Quinn, p. 60; and Richard Moody, ed., *Dramas from the American Theatre, 1762–1909* (Cleveland: World Publishing Co., 1966), p. xii.

70. A Whig of '76 was one who belonged to the independence party during the Revolution.

71. This correspondent is referring to the fact that Ioor's first play was a comedy and that John Blake White's *Foscari* (first produced in 1806) was a tragedy.

72. Organization formed by the officers of the Continental Army after the Revolution.

Chapter IV

1. *The National Cyclopaedia of American Biography* (New York: James T. White, 1893-1965), III, 21.

2. Mabel L. Webber, ed., "Records from the Blake and White Bibles" in the *South Carolina Historical and Genealogical Magazine*, 36 (July, 1935), 19. References to this source will hereafter be labeled "Family Bibles."

3. Paul W. Partridge, Jr., "John Blake White: Southern Romantic Painter and Playwright," Diss. Univ. of Pennsylvania 1951, pp. 5-6. I am much indebted to his study, the most complete account of White's life available.

4. Letter of Thomas G. White, son of John Blake White, to Henry Buist, April 25, 1909, quoted by Partridge, p. 5; Partridge, p. 9.

5. "Family Bibles," *SCHGM*, 36 (April, 1935), 42.

6. Paul R. Weidner, ed., "The Journal of John Blake White," *SCHGM*, 42 (April, 1941), 61; (July, 1941), 99, 109. This journal is held by the South Carolina Historical Society, Charleston. Subsequent references will be labeled "Journal."

7. Partridge, p. 29, citing Eugen Neuhaus, *The History and Ideals of American Art* (Stanford University, Calif., 1931), p. 23.

8. "Journal," *SCHGM*, 42, (April, 1941), 68, n.; (July, 1941), 111.

9. Ibid., *SCHGM*, 42 (July, 1941), 104, 107.

10. "Family Bibles," *SCHGM*, 36 (April, 1935), 43. See Beatrice St. Julien Ravenel, *Architects of Charleston* (Charleston: R. L. Bryan, 1945).

11. The "Cash Book" is in the possession of the South Carolina Historical Society; "Journal," *SCHGM*, 43 (April, 1942), 110.

12. John Blake White, *Foscari* (Charleston: J. Hoff, 1806). The best known version of this tragedy is Byron's *The Two Foscari* (1821).

13. John Blake White, *The Mysteries of the Castle* (Charleston: J. Hoff, 1807), prologue.

14. Oral Sumner Coad, "The Gothic Element in American Literature Before 1835," *Journal of English and Germanic Philology*, 24 (1925), 76.

15. John Blake White, *Modern Honor* (Charleston: J. Hoff, 1812); *The Triumph of Liberty* (Charleston: J. Hoff, 1819); *The Forgers* in the *Southern Literary Journal*, 1 (1837), Nos. 2, 3, 4, 5, 6.

16. John Blake White, "An Oration . . . in Commemoration of the Adoption of the Federal Constitution" (Charleston: *Southern Patriot*, 1815).

17. Partridge, p. 85.

18. Anna Wells Rutledge, "Artists in the Life of Charleston," *American Philosophical Transactions*, 39, Part 2 (Philadelphia, 1949), p. 136; Partridge, p. 88, citing John L. E. W. Shecut, *Medical and Philosophical Essays, Containing . . . Sketches of Charleston . . . to Present* (Charleston, 1819), p. 52.

19. Linda Rhea, *Hugh Swinton Legaré* (Chapel Hill: Univ. of North Carolina Press, 1934), p. 70.

20. Partridge, pp. 90, 96.

21. *Courier*, Feb. 6, 1819.

22. "Journal," *SCHGM*, 43 (July, 1942), 174.

23. "Journal," *SCHGM*, 43 (July, 1942), 168-169; "Family Bibles," *SCHGM*, 36 (Oct., 1935), 114.

24. Partridge, p. 126, "Family Bibles," *SCHGM*, 36 (July, 1935), 93; (Oct., 1935), 120.

25. "Family Bibles," *SCHGM*, 36 (Oct., 1935), 120.

26. "Journal," *SCHGM*, 43 (April, 1942), 107; "Family Bibles," *SCHGM*, 36 (Oct., 1935), 121.

27. See "Our Early Authors and Artists," *XIX Century*, 1 (Sept., 1869), 279.

28. Partridge, p. 94.

29. Its longer title is "A scene of Grave Robbers in affright by the reanimation of a Lady whose Tomb they had entered to despoil of her jewels."

30. In the possession of the South Carolina Historical Society. Another Charlestonian of White's time who combined interests in painting and literature was the poet James M. Legaré. See Curtis Carroll Davis, *That Ambitious Mr. Legaré* (Columbia: Univ. of South Carolina Press, 1971), pp. 30, 132.

31. This portrait was inherited by George Lamb Buist, Sparta, N. J., and is now in his possesion. Partridge, p. 79.

32. *Courier*, March 26, 1825.

33. "Reports and Resolutions of the South Carolina Legislature," in the *Courier*, Dec. 6, 1825; Partridge, p. 94.

34. Partridge, p. 124.

35. "On the Intellectual and Moral Relations of the Fine Arts," *Southern Literary Journal*, 1 (Aug., 1837), 488-489, n., cited by Partridge, p. 152.

36. The letter is in the possession of the Historical Society of Pennsylvania.

37. J. F. Rippy, *Joel R. Poinsett, Versatile Statesman* (Durham: Duke Univ. Press, 1935), p. 226.

38. The notes are fully described in Washington A. Clark, *The History of the Banking Institutions Organized in South Carolina Prior to 1860* (Columbia: Historical Commission of South Carolina, 1922), p. 300, cited by Partridge, p. 171. Engravings of this painting are also held by the South Carolina Historical Society, Gibbes Art Gallery, and B. Allston Moore.

39. Partridge, pp. 171-173.

40. Rutledge, p. 136.

41. This letter is in the possession of the Historical Society of Pennsylvania. Robert Milledge Charlton was judge of the Superior Court of Georgia, U. S. senator, and mayor of Savannah. *Who Was Who in America, 1607-1897* (Chicago: A. N. Marquis, 1963).

42. Partridge, p. 193.

43. The former is now lost; the latter is in the private collection of Mrs. William L. Clements, Bay City, Michigan, according to Partridge, p. 198.

44. *Dictionary of American Biography;* Partridge, p. 9.

45. *The Vindication: A Satire, on "Charleston: A Poem"* (Charleston, 1848), p. 26. The author was Augustin Louis Taveau, an Edisto rice planter and contributor to Charleston newspapers and magazines. See *The Letters of William Gilmore Simms,* ed. Mary C. Simms Oliphant, Alfred Taylor Odell, and T. C. Duncan Eaves (Columbia: Univ. of South Carolina Press, 1952-1956), II, 463. A copy of this booklet is held by the Univ. of North Carolina Library.

46. White was in fact twenty-four when his first play was presented in 1806.

47. *The Mysteries of the Castle.*

48. The Revolutionary heroes are Generals Francis Marion, William Moultrie, Thomas Sumter, and Colonel Henry Lee.

49. A laudatory letter from England to White was described in the *Courier*, Oct 5, 1848.

50. Letter in the possession of the Historical Society of Pennsylvania.

51. Partridge, p. 174; White's will is held by the South Carolina Archives Department, Columbia. *Records of Wills,* Vol. 48A, Book M, 1856-62, Charleston County.

52. "Proceedings of the Council, Tuesday, June 4, 1839" in the *Courier,* June 7, 1839, cited by Partridge, p. 189.

53. Partridge, pp. 202-203.

54. *Courier*, Aug. 25, 1859.

55. Partridge, p. 213.

56. C. B. Galbreath, "Thomas Smith Grimké," *Ohio Archaeological and Historical Publications,*" 33 (1924), 309.

57. Cited by Josef A. Elfenbein, "American Drama, 1782-1812, as an Index to Socio-Political Thought," Diss. New York Univ., 1952. p. 243.

58. Ibid., p. 245.

59. William Lucas, *The Duellists; or Men of Honour: a story; calculated to show the folly, extravagance, and sin of duelling* (London: J. Cundee, 1805).

60. William Oliver Stevens, *Pistols at Ten Paces: The Story of the Code of Honor in America* (Boston: Houghton, Mifflin, 1940), p. 31.

61. Ibid., p. 33.

62. Clement Eaton, *Freedom of Thought in the Old South* (Durham: Duke Univ. Press, 1940), p. 53.

63. Stevens, p. 92.

64. Eaton, p. 53.

65. Stevens, p. 92.

66. David Duncan Wallace, *South Carolina: A Short History, 1520-1948* (Chapel Hill: Univ. of North Carolina Press, 1951), pp. 493-494.

67. "Journal," *SCHGM,* 43 (July, 1942), 167-168.

68. John Blake White, *Modern Honor* (Charleston: J. Hoff, 1812).

69: There was disapproval of duels between military officers and civilians. Andrew Jackson, a duelist himself, opposed them when he became president. See Stevens, p. 51.

70. "Journal," *SCHGM,* 43 (April, 1942), 111-112.

71. In possession of the South Carolina Historical Society.

72. [William Gilmore Simms, ed.], *The Charleston Book: A Miscellany in Prose and Verse* (Charleston: S. Hart, 1845), pp. 126, 128, 130-132.

73. This play was first entitled "Mordaunt, or the Victim of Intemperance," as shown by the manuscript dated 1829, now in the possession of the South Carolina Historical Society. *The Forgers* was published in the *Southern Literary Journal,* 1 (1837), Nos. 2, 3, 4, 5, 6.

74. Donald A. Koch, ed., *Ten Nights in a Bar-Room and What I Saw There by Timothy Shaw Arthur* (Cambridge, Mass: Belknap Press, 1964), pp. xlix, li, liv.

75. Richard Moody, *Dramas from the American Theatre, 1762-1909* (Cleveland: World Publishing Co., 1966), p. 279; Koch, p. lxxx.

76. Wallace, pp. 410-411.

77. Eaton, p. 323.

78. John Evans Eubanks, *Ben Tillman's Baby; The Dispensary System of South Carolina, 1892-1915* (n.p., [1950]), p. 39; Wallace, p. 491; Eaton, p. 323.

79. Wallace, pp. 490-491.

80. Henry Anselm Scomp, *King Alcohol in the Realm of King Cotton.*

Or, a History of the liquor traffic and of the temperance movement in Georgia, from 1733 to 1887 ([Chicago]: Blakely Printing Co., 1888), p. 301.

81. In the possession of the South Carolina Historical Society.

82. This letter is in the possession of the South Carolina Historical Society. White's correspondent is most probably Edmund Trowbridge Dana. He had met him in England and referred to him as "my old and valued Friend" in a letter dated Feb. 19, 1844, to Richard Henry Dana, Sr., the poet and editor (in the possession of the Massachusetts Historical Society). For references to Edmund Trowbridge Dana, see Edgar P. Richardson, *Washington Allston* (Chicago: Univ. of Chicago Press, 1948), pp. 89, 90; and H. W. L. Dana, *The Dana Saga, Three Centuries of the Dana Family in Cambridge* (Cambridge, Mass.: Cambridge Historical Society, 1941), p. 36.

83. Pelby, manager of the Tremont Theatre in Boston, had offered a prize of five hundred dollars for the best tragedy. See Arthur Hobson Quinn, *A History of the American Drama from the Beginning to the Civil War* (New York: Appleton-Century-Crofts, 1943), p. 264.

84. *Southern Literary Journal*, 1 (April, 1837), 190.

85. John Blake White, *The Triumph of Liberty* (Charleston: J. Hoff, 1819).

86. Two studies which examine systematically the political purposes of early American plays are J. Elfenbein, "American Drama, 1782-1812, as an Index to Socio-Political Thought," Diss. New York Univ., 1952, and Norman Philbrick, *Trumpets Sounding: Propaganda Plays of the American Revolution* (New York: Benjamin Blom, 1972).

87. George Dangerfield, *The Awakening of American Nationalism, 1815-1828* (New York: Harper and Row, 1965), pp. 38, 45, 49-50.

88. Samuel Eliot Morrison and Henry Steele Commager, *The Growth of the American Republic* (New York: Oxford Univ. Press, 1950), I, 451.

89. Marquis James, *The Life of Andrew Jackson* (Indianapolis: Bobbs Merril, 1938), p. 298.

90. *The Life and Speeches of Henry Clay*, ed. James B. Swain (Philadelphia: J. L. Gihon, 1854), I, 136.

91. J. S. Bassett, *The Life of Andrew Jackson* (New York: Macmillan, 1928), pp. 270-271; James, pp. 298-299.

92. Bassett, pp. 291-292.

93. "Journal," *SCHGM*, 43 (July, 1942), 173, 174.

94. White probably used as a source for his play *The Life of Andrew Jackson* by John Henry Eaton and John Reid (Philadelphia: M. Carey and Son, 1817). Descriptions of American preparations for the battle in both works are given in similar language.

95. Bassett, pp. 255, 256, 258.

96. *American State Papers, Foreign Relations*, (Washington, 1832-1861), IV, 540.

97. James, p. 289.
98. Ibid., p. 286.
99. Bassett, p. 254.
100. Dangerfield, pp. 44-45.
101. Bassett, p. 256.
102. Dangerfield, p. 45.
103. White's attitude toward Indian attacks had been shown earlier. He wrote that during the War of 1812, he completed a painting entitled "The Massacre of the American Prisoners by the English and their Indian allies at french town, on the River Raisin." See "Journal," *SCHGM*, 43 (April, 1942), 117.
104. Ludwig Lewisohn, "Books We have Made, A History of Literature in South Carolina," Charleston *News and Courier*, Sunday News, July 5-Sept. 20, 1903, Part III; Quinn, pp. 188-190.

Chapter V

1. *The Letters of William Gilmore Simms*, ed. Mary C. Simms Oliphant, et al. (Columbia: Univ. of South Carolina Press, 1952-56), III, 280, n., hereafter designated *Letters*. The essay appeared in *The Orion*, 4 (March, 1844), 41-51; (April, 1844), 76-89; (May, 1844), 105-119; (June, 1844), 179-194.
2. C. Hugh Holman, "Simms and the British Dramatists,' *PMLA*, 65 (June, 1950), 351-355.
3. See Edward P. Vandiver, Jr., "Simms's Border Romances and Shakespeare," *Shakespeare Quarterly*, 5 (Spring, 1954), 132-134.
4. *Woodcraft* (New York: W. W. Norton, 1961), p. 53.
5. *The Yemassee*, ed. C. Hugh Holman (Cambridge, Mass.: Houghton, Mifflin, 1961), p. 6.
6. "Dr. Irving's Reminiscences of the Charleston Stage," ed. Emmett Robinson, *SCHGM*, 52 (1951), 166.
7. W. Stanley Hoole, "Charleston Theatres," *Southwest Review*, 25 (Jan., 1940), 197.
8. From an article on the theatre written by Simms in *Southern Literary Journal*, n. s., 1 (May, 1837), 232, 235-237, cited by Miriam J. Shillingsburg, "Simms's Review of Shakespeare on the Stage," *Tennessee Studies in Literature*, 16 (1971), 123-124.
9. Hoole, *The Ante-bellum Charleston Theatre* (Tuscaloosa: Univ. of Alabama Press, 1946), p. 40.
10. "Our Early Authors and Artists," *XIX Century*, 1 (Sept., 1869), 279.
11. "Battle of Fort Moultrie," *Southern Literary Gazette* (1829), p. 132.
12. *Letters*, I, 194.

13. "Our Early Authors and Artists," *XIX Century,* 1 (Sept., 1869), 279.

14. Ibid., pp. 279-280.

15. *XIX Century,* 2 (Jan., 1870), 633. This review appeared "twenty or more years ago," according to [Yates Snowden], *South Carolina Plays and Playwrights* (Columbia, S.C., 1909), p. 7.

16. Ibid., p. 636.

17. Ibid., (Sept. 1869), p. 287.

18. *Letters,* I, 285.

19. James W. Dewsnap, "William Gilmore Simms as Playwright," Diss. Univ. of Georgia, 1971, p. 51.

20. Ibid., pp. 54-55.

21. *Letters,* I, cv.

22. Ibid., I, 45. The tragedy is unidentified.

23. Richard Moody, *Edwin Forrest* (New York: Alfred Knopf, 1960), pp. 88-91.

24. *Letters,* I, 185-186, 189.

25. *Border Beagles* (New York: Redfield, 1855), p. 80.

26. *Letters,* I, 187-188.

27. Ibid., I, 427.

28. Dewsnap, p. 101.

29. *Sartain's Magazine* (April, 1851), pp. 249-253. See Dewsnap, p. 111.

30. Dewsnap, p. 111.

31. *Letters,* II, 214.

32. Ibid., II, 346, 350.

33. Ibid., II, 357.

34. Ibid., II, 369. "Arnold" is his dramatic poem "Benedict Arnold."

35. This two volume collection was published first by John Russell, Charleston, and then in the same year by Redfield.

36. Dewsnap, p. 32.

37. *Letters,* III, 163.

38. Dewsnap, pp. 38-39.

39. *Letters,* III, 202, 215.

40. Ibid., III, 193.

41. Ibid., III, 7, n.

42. Ibid., II, 460; III, 7, n.

43. Ibid., I, 388.

44. Cited by Montrose J. Moses, *The Fabulous Forrest* (Boston: Little, Brown and Co., 1929), p. 111.

45. *Letters,* I, 404.

46. Ibid., I, 407.

47. Ibid., II, 214.

48. Ibid., pp. 367-368.

49. For his use of this expression, see *Letters,* IV, 532, and V, 100.

50. *Southern Literary Messenger,* 18 (February, 1852), 89. All quotations from the play are from this edition, which appeared from February through June, 1852.

51. W. Stanley Hoole, "Simms's *Michael Bonham,* a Forgotten Drama of the Texas Revolution," *Southwest Historical Quarterly,* 46 (Jan., 1942), 261. See also Milledge Bonham, Jr., "James Butler Bonham: A Consistent Rebel," *Southwest Historical Quarterly,* 35 (Oct., 1931), 129.

52. *Letters,* III, 372-373.

53. William P. Trent, *William Gilmore Simms* (Boston: Houghton, Mifflin, 1892), pp. 216-217.

54. Hammond Papers, Library of Congress. quoted in *Letters,* III, 373, n.

55. *Letters,* III, 372, n.

56. Hoole, *Ante-bellum Charleston Theatre,* p. 138. The acting manager, like today's stage manager, superintended a performance.

57. Hoole, "Simms's *Michael Bonham,*" p. 256.

58. Cited by Hoole, ibid., pp. 256-257.

59. *Letters,* III, 372-373, n.

60. Arthur Hobson Quinn, *A History of the American Drama from the Beginning to the Civil War* (New York: Appleton-Century-Crofts, 1943), p. 445.

61. Jon L. Wakelyn, *The Politics of a Literary Man: William Gilmore Simms* (Westport, Conn.: Greenwood Press, 1973), p. 89. Southerners' support of westward expansion as a means of defending the slave society has been emphasized by Eugene D. Genovese, *The Political Economy of Slavery* (1965; rpt., New York: Pantheon, 1967), pp. 243-274.

62. *Confession* (New York: Redfield, 1856), pp. 205-207.

63. Wakelyn, pp. 91-92.

64. *Letters,* II, 23-24.

65. Ibid., I, 446, n.

66. Wakelyn, p. 201.

67. Ibid., p. 164.

68. "Calhoun.—An Ode." printed at the end of "Charleston, The Palmetto City," *Harper's New Monthly Magazine,* 15 (Jan., 1857), 22.

69. Ibid.

70. *Letters,* II, 341.

71. Ibid., II, 346.

72. Ibid., II, 350.

73. Ibid., II, 359.

74. Ibid., II, 368-369.

75. Ibid., II, 369.

76. *International Magazine,* 4 (October 1, 1851), 412, cited in *Letters,* III, 146, n.

77. *Literary World,* 9 (Sept. 20, 1852), 223, cited in *Letters,* III, 153, n.

78. *Graham's* 46 (May, 1854), 546.
79. *Letters*, III, 169, n.
80. Ibid., III, 203, n.
81. "The Dramatic Poems of William Gilmore Simms," *Russell's Magazine*, 2 (Dec., 1857), 240-259.
82. *Letters*, III, 161.
83. Ibid., III, 162-163. Adams was manager of the Charleston Theatre, January-April, 1850, and October-December, 1850. See Hoole, *The Antebellum Charleston Theatre*, pp. 53-57.
84. Trent, p. 200.
85. Moses, pp. 166-167.
86. Richard Moody, *Edwin Forrest* (New York: Alfred Knopf, 1960), p. 171.
87. Ibid., pp. 270, 279.
88. Cited by Moody, p. 175.
89. Moody, p. 176.
90. Ibid., pp. 176-177.
91. Ibid., p. 177.
92. Ibid., p. 177.
93. *Norman Maurice; or The Man of the People* in *Poems: Descriptive, Dramatic, Legendary and Contemplative*, I (New York: Redfield, 1853), Act II, Scene 5. All references are to this edition and are hereafter given in the text.
94. Edwin C. McReynolds, *Missouri, A History of the Crossroads State* (Norman: Univ. of Oklahoma Press, [1962]), p. 172.
95. *Dictionary of American Biography, sub nomine*.
96. *Letters*, II, 4.
97. Ibid., II, 321-322.
98. Wakelyn, p. 164.
99. See for example *Charlemont* (New York: Redfield, 1856), pp. 31, 237 and the titles for chapters 4 ("Simplicity and the Serpent"), 6, and 26. For a discussion of this imagery, see W. B. Gates, "William Gilmore Simms and the Kentucky Tragedy," *American Literature*, 32 (May, 1960), 163-164.
100. *Egeria, or Voices of Thought and Comfort for the Woods and Wayside* (Philadelphia: E. A. Butler and Co., 1853); *Joscelyn* (New York: *The Old Guard*, 1867).
101. *Letters*, II, 131.
102. Elizabeth Merritt, *James Henry Hammond, 1807-1864* (Baltimore: The Johns Hopkins Press, 1923), p. 80.
103. *Letters*, IV, 105-106.

Chapter VI

1. Martin S. Shockley, "American Plays in the Richmond Theatre,

172   Notes

1819-1838," *Studies in Philology*, 37 (1940), 109-110.

2. The plays by Robert Munford have been republished in the *William and Mary Quarterly*, 5 and 6 (April, 1948), 217-257, and (July, 1949), 437-502. Those by William Munford and Burk have been reproduced in microprint in *Three Centuries of English and American Plays*. The play by Wirt is not extant. For a discussion of his play, see Frank P. Cauble, "William Wirt and His Friends: A Study in Southern Culture" (Diss., Univ. of North Carolina, 1933), 256-260. Tucker's play exists in a manuscript held by Colonial Williamsburg. It has been reproduced in "A Critical Edition of St. George Tucker's 'The Wheel of Fortune,'" by Hal Laughlin (Master's thesis, College of William and Mary, 1960).

3. Arthur Hobson Quinn, *A History of the American Drama from the Beginning to the Civil War* (New York: Appleton-Century-Crofts, 1943), p. 430.

4. Joseph Patrick Roppolo, "American Themes, Heroes and History on the New Orleans Stage, 1806-1865," *Tulane Studies in English*, 5 (1955), 166.

5. Joseph Patrick Roppolo, "Local and Topical Plays in New Orleans, 1806-1865," *Tulane Studies in English*, 4 (1954), 115.

6. Ibid., p. 91.

7. Ibid., p. 115.

8. Ibid., p. 110.

9. Ibid., p. 95.

10. Ibid., pp. 98-99.

11. Ibid., p. 109.

12. Ibid., p. 94.

13. Quinn, p. 140.

14. Ibid., p. 251.

15. Ibid., p. 229.

16. Ibid., p. 349.

17. Ibid., p. 170.

18. Ibid., pp. 178-180.

19. Ibid., pp. 434, 428, 430.

20. Ibid., p. 291.

Appendix

1. All performances were in Charleston unless otherwise specified. Charleston productions have been checked in W. Stanley Hoole, *The Antebellum Charleston Theatre* and the *Courier*.

2. In addition, an unknown number in New York and Philadelphia.

SELECT BIBLIOGRAPHY

I. Primary Sources

Note: All the plays listed in "Primary Sources" except John Blake White's *Triumph of Liberty* and *The Forgers* and William Gilmore Simms's plays are reproduced on microprint in the collection *Three Centuries of Drama: American.*

Americana; or, A New Tale of the Genii. Baltimore: W. Pechin, 1802.

Beete, John. *The Man of the Times: or, A Scarcity of Cash. A Farce.* Charleston: W. P. Young, [1797].

Crafts, William. *The Sea-Serpent.* Charleston: A. E. Miller, 1819.

The Female Enthusiast: A Tragedy in Five Acts. Charleston: J. Hoff, 1807.

Harby, Isaac. *Alberti* in *Selections from the Miscellaneous Writings of the Late Isaac Harby,* ed. Henry L. Pinckney and Abraham Moise. Charleston: James S. Burges, 1829.

————. *The Gordian Knot.* Charleston: G. M. Bounetheau, 1810.

Holland, E. C. *The Corsair.* Charleston: A. E. Miller, 1818.

Ioor, William. *The Battle of the Eutaw Springs and Evacuation of Charleston ; or The Glorious 14th of December, 1782.* Charleston: J. Hoff, 1807. (I have chosen to use the shorter title, *The Battle of Eutaw Springs,* as have others, in referring to the play.)

————. *Independence.* Charleston: G. M. Bounetheau, 1805.

Pinckney, Maria. *The Young Carolinians; or, Americans in Algiers* in *Essays, Religious, Moral Dramatic and Poetical.* Charleston: A. E. Miller, 1818.

Simmons, James Wright. *Manfredi.* Philadelphia: Moses Thomas, 1821.

————. *Valdemar; or, The Castle of the Cliff.* Philadelphia: H. C. Carey and I. Lea, 1822.

Simms, William Gilmore. *Michael Bonham; or, The Fall of Bexar* in *Southern Literary Messenger,* 18 (Feb.-June, 1852), 89-96, 145-149, 234-240, 296-304, 342-349.

————. *Norman Maurice; or, The Man of the People* in *Poems: Descriptive, Dramatic, Legendary, and Contemplative,* I. New York: Redfield, 1853. 2 v. (The title of these volumes is given as *Poems* after its first appearance in the text.)

White, John Blake. *The Forgers* in the *Southern Literary Journal,* 1

173

(April, May, June, July, August, 1837), 118-125, 218-226, 354-362, 435-443, 509-518.

————. *The Forgers; A Dramatic Poem.* Reprinted from the *Southern Literary Journal* of 1837 by order of his son, Octavius A. White, 1899.

————. *Foscari.* Charleston: J. Hoff, 1806. (Two manuscript copies of this play, dated 1805 and 1806, are in the possession of the South Carolina Historical Society.)

————. *Modern Honor.* Charleston: J. Hoff, 1812. (A manuscript copy of this play, dated 1811, is in the possession of the South Carolina Historical Society.)

————. *The Mysteries of the Castle.* Charleston: J. Hoff, 1807.

————. *The Triumph of Liberty, or Louisiana Preserved.* Charleston: J. Hoff, 1819. (A copy is in the possession of The Library Company of Philadelphia, Pa.)

Workman, James. *Liberty in Louisiana.* Charleston: Query and Evans, 1804.

II. Secondary Sources

Abernethy, Thomas P. *The South in the New Nation, 1789-1819.* Baton Rouge: Louisiana State Univ. Press, 1961.

American Literary Manuscripts. Austin: Univ. of Texas Press, 1961.

Baine, Rodney M. *Robert Munford: America's First Comic Dramatist.* Athens: Univ. of Georgia Press, 1967.

Bass, Robert Duncan. "The Plays and Playwrights of South Carolina." Master's thesis, Univ. of South Carolina, 1927.

Bergquist, G. William, ed. *Three Centuries of English and American Plays: A Checklist. England: 1500-1800, United States: 1714-1830.* New York: Hafner, 1963. (This is the checklist for *Three Centuries of Drama: American.*)

Bernheim, Alfred L. *The Business of the Theatre; An Economic History of the American Theatre, 1750-1932.* New York: B. Blom, 1964.

Bowes, Frederick P. *The Culture of Early Charleston.* Chapel Hill: Univ. of North Carolina Press, 1942.

Brockett, O. G. "The European Career of Alexander Placide." *Southern Speech Journal,* 27 (Summer, 1962), 306-313.

————. The Theatre of the Southern United States from the Beginnings Through 1865: A Bibliographical Essay." *Theatre Research,* 2, (1960), 163-174.

Cardwell, Guy A. "Charleston Periodicals, 1795-1860: A Study in Literary Influences, with a Descriptive Check List of Seventy-Five Magazines." Diss. Univ. of North Carolina, 1933.

Charvat, William. *The Origins of American Critical Thought, 1810-1835.* Philadelphia: Univ. of Pennsylvania Press, 1936.

Chevalley, Sylvie. "The Death of Alexander Placide." *South Carolina*

Historical and Genealogical Magazine, 58 (April, 1957), 63-66.

Clark, Thomas D., ed. *Travels in the Old South: A Bibliography*, II. *The Expanding South, 1750-1825*. Norman, Okla.: Univ. of Oklahoma Press, 1956.

Curtis, Julia. "The Architecture and Appearance of the Charleston Theatre, 1793-1833." *Educational Theatre Journal*, 23 (1971), 1-12.

————. "The Early Charleston Stage: 1703-1798." Diss. Indiana Univ. 1968.

David, Richard Beale. *Intellectual Life in Jefferson's Virginia, 1798-1830*. Chapel Hill: Univ. of North Carolina Press, 1964.

Dewsnap, James William. "William Gilmore Simms as Playwright." Diss. Univ. of Georgia, 1971.

Dictionary of American Biography, 20 vols. New York: C. Scribner's Sons, 1928-1936.

Dormon, James H., Jr. *Theatre in the Ante Bellum South, 1815-1861*. Chapel Hill: Univ. of North Carolina Press, 1967.

Drayton, John. *A View of South Carolina, as respects her natural and civil concerns*. Charleston: W. P. Young, 1802.

Dunlap, William. *History of the American Theatre* (1832). Reprint, New York: Burt Franklin, 1963.

Duyckinck, Evert A. and Duyckinck, George L. *Cyclopaedia of American Literature*. 2 vols. Philadelphia: William Rutter, 1877.

Eaton, Clement. *Freedom of Thought in the Old South*. Durham: Duke Univ. Press, 1940.

Elfenbein, Josef. "American Drama, 1782-1812, as an Index to Socio-Political Thought." Diss. New York Univ., 1952.

Galbreath, C. B. "Thomas Smith Grimké." *Ohio Archaeological and Historical Publications*, 33 (1924), 301-312.

Gohdes, Clarence L. F. *Literature and Theatre of the States and Regions of the U. S. A.; an historical bibliography*. Durham: Duke Univ. Press, 1967.

Gray, Lewis Cecil. *History of Agriculture in the Southern United States to 1860*. 2 vols. Washington: Carnegie Institute of Washington, 1933.

Harby, Isaac. *A Selection from the Miscellaneous Writings of the Late Isaac Harby*, ed. Henry L. Pinckney and Abraham Moise with "A Memoir of His Life," by Abraham Moise. Charleston: James S. Burges, 1829.

Hayne, Paul Hamilton. "The Dramatic Poems of William Gilmore Simms." *Russell's Magazine*, 2 (Dec., 1857), 240-259.

Hill, Frank P. *American Plays, Printed, 1714-1830*. Stanford, Calif.: Stanford University Press, 1934.

Holman, C. Hugh. "Simms and the British Dramatists." *PMLA*, 65 (June, 1950), 351-355.

Hoole, W. Stanley. *The Ante-bellum Charleston Theatre*, Tuscaloosa: Univ. of Alabama Press, 1946.

————. "Charleston Theatres," *Southwest Review,* 25 (Jan., 1940), 193-204.

————. "Shakespeare on the Antebellum Charleston Stage," *Shakespeare Association Bulletin,* 21 (Jan., 1946), 37-45.

————. "Simms's *Michael Bonham,* A 'Forgotten Drama' of the Texas Revolution," *Southwest Historical Quarterly,* 46 (Jan., 1942), 255-261.

Hornblow, Arthur. *A History of the Theatre in America from Its Beginnings to the Present Time.* 2 vols. Philadelphia: J. B. Lippincott, 1919.

Hubbell, Jay. B. *The South in American Literature, 1607-1900.* Durham: Duke Univ. Press, 1954.

Hughes, Glenn. *A History of the American Theatre, 1700-1950.* New York: Samuel French, 1951.

Johnson, Guion Griffis. *Ante-bellum North Carolina, A Social History.* Chapel Hill: Univ. of North Carolina Press, 1937.

King, William L. *The Newspaper Press of Charleston, S. C.* Charleston: Edward Perry, 1872.

Leiding, Harriette Kershaw. *Charleston: Historic and Romantic.* Philadelphia: J. B. Lippincott, 1931.

Lewisohn, Ludwig. "Books We Have Made, A History of Literature in South Carolina." Charleston *News and Courier,* Sunday News, July 5-September 20, 1903.

Library of Southern Literature, ed. Edwin Anderson Alderman, et al. 16 vols. New Orleans: Martin and Hoyt, 1908-1913.

Litto, Frederic M. *American Dissertations of the Drama and the Theatre: A Bibliography.* Kent, Ohio: Kent State Univ. Press, 1969.

Maxwell, William Bulloch. *The Mysterious Father,* ed. Gerald Kahan. Athens: Univ. of Georgia Press, 1965. (This first play of Georgia was published in 1807.)

Meserve, Walter J. "The American Periodical Series: Source Material for Theatre and Drama Research." *Educational Theatre Journal,* 20 (Oct., 1968), 443-448.

Moise, L. C. *Biography of Isaac Harby.* (The date of publication has been determined to be 1931. No other facts are known.)

Moody, Richard. *America Takes the Stage: Romanticism in American Drama and Theatre, 1750-1909.* Bloomington, Ind.: Indiana Univ. Press, 1955.

Moody, Richard. *Dramas from the American Theatre, 1762-1909.* Cleveland: World Publishing Co., 1966.

Moore, John Hammond. *Research Materials in South Carolina, a Guide compiled and edited for the South Carolina Library Board.* Columbia: Univ. of South Carolina Press, 1967.

Moses, Montrose J. *The American Dramatist.* Boston: Little, Brown, 1925.

————. *The Literature of the South.* New York: T. Y. Crowell, 1910.

————. *Representative Plays by American Dramatists.* 3 vols. New York: E. P. Dutton, 1918-1925.

Munford, Robert. *The Candidates; or The Humours of a Virginia Election*, ed. Jay B. Hubbell and Douglass Adair. *William and Mary Quarterly*, Third Series, 5 (April, 1948), 217-257. (This first play of Virginia was published in 1798.)

————. *The Patriots*, ed. Courtlandt Canby. *William and Mary Quarterly*, Third Series, 6 (July, 1949), 437-502. (First published in 1798.)

The National Cyclopaedia of American Biography. New York: James T. White, 1893-1965.

Nicoll, Allardyce. *British Drama*. London: George G. Harrap, 1932.

————. *A History of English Drama*. Vol. III: *Late Eighteenth Century Drama, 1750-1800*. Cambridge, England: The University Press, 1961.

————. *A History of English Drama*. Vol. IV: *Early Nineteenth Century Drama, 1800-1850*. Cambridge, England: The University Press, 1960.

Nye, Russell. *The Cultural Life of the New Nation, 1776-1830*. New York: Harper and Row, 1960.

Odell, George C. D. *Annals of the New York Stage*. 13 vols. New York: Columbia Univ. Press, 1927-1942.

O'Neall, J. B. *Biographical Sketches of the Bench and Bar of South Carolina*. 2 vols. Charleston: Courtenay and Co., 1859.

Parks, Edd Winfield. *Segments of Southern Thought*. Athens: Univ. of Georgia Press, 1938.

————. *William Gilmore Simms as Literary Critic*. Athens: Univ. of Georgia Press, 1961.

Parrington, Vernon Louis. *Main Currents in American Thought*. 3 vols. New York: Harcourt, Brace, 1927-1930.

Partridge, Paul W., Jr. "John Blake White: Southern Romantic Painter and Playwright." Diss. in American Civilization, Univ. of Pennsylvania, 1951.

Philips, Ulrich Bonnell. *Life and Labor in the Old South*. Boston: Little, Brown, 1929.

Patrick, J. Max. *Savannah's Pioneer Theatre from Its Origins to 1810*. Athens: Univ. of Georgia Press, 1953.

Pinckney, Maria Henrietta. *A Notice of the Pinckneys*. Charleston: Evans and Cogswell, 1860.

Quinn, Arthur Hobson. *A History of the American Drama from the Beginning to the Civil War*. New York: Appleton-Century-Crofts, 1943.

————. *Representative American Plays: From 1767 to the Present Day*. New York: Appleton-Century-Crofts, 1953.

Ramsay, David. *The History of South-Carolina, from its first settlement in 1670 to the year 1808*. 2 vols. Charleston: David Longworth, 1809.

Rankin, Hugh S. *The Theater in Colonial America*. Chapel Hill: Univ. of North Carolina Press, 1965.

Ravenel, Harriott Horry. *Charleston. The Place and the People*. New York: Macmillan, 1906.

Rhea, Linda. *Hugh Swinton Legaré.* Chapel Hill: Univ. of North Carolina Press, 1934.

Richardson, Edgar P. *Washington Allston.* Chicago: Univ. of Chicago Press, 1948.

Rippy, J. F. *Joel R. Poinsett, Versatile Statesman.* Durham: Duke Univ. Press, 1935.

Robinson, Emmett, ed. "Dr. Irving's Reminiscences of the Charleston Stage." *South Carolina Historical and Genealogical Magazine,* 51 (July, Oct., 1950), 125-131, 195-215; 52 (Jan., April, July, Oct., 1951), 26-33, 93-106, 166-179, 225-232; 53 (Jan., 1952), 37-47.

Rogers, George C., Jr. *Charleston in the Age of the Pinckneys.* Norman: Univ. of Oklahoma Press, 1969.

————. *A South Carolina Chronology 1497-1970.* Columbia: Univ. of South Carolina Press, 1973.

Roppolo, Joseph Patrick. "American Themes, Heroes and History on the New Orleans Stage, 1806-1865." *Tulane Studies in English,* 5 (1955), 151-181.

————. "Local and Topical Plays in New Orleans, 1806-1865." *Tulane Studies in English,* 4 (1954), 91-124.

Rutledge, Anna Wells. *Artists in the Life of Charleston, American Philosophical Transactions,* Vol. 39, Part 2. Philadelphia, 1949.

————. *Catalogue of Paintings and Sculpture in the Council Chamber, City Hall, Charleston, South Carolina.* Copyright by the City Council of Charleston, 1943.

Sabin, Joseph. *Bibliotheca Americana.* 29 vols. New York, 1868-1938.

Sass, Herbert Ravenel. *Outspoken, 150 Years of the News and Courier.* Columbia: Univ. of South Carolina Press, 1953.

Sherman, Susanne K. "Thomas Wade West, Theatrical Impresario, 1790-1799." *William and Mary Quarterly,* Third Series, 9 (Jan., 1952), 10-28.

Shillingsburg, Miriam J. "Simms's Review of Shakespeare on the Stage." *Tennessee Studies in Literature,* 16 (1971), 121-135.

Shockley, Martin Staples. "American Plays in the Richmond Theatre, 1819-1838." *Studies in Philology,* 37 (1940), 100-119.

————. "A History of the Theatre in Richmond, Virginia, 1819-1838." Diss. Univ. of North Carolina, 1938.

[Simms, William Gilmore, ed.] *The Charleston Book: A Miscellany in Prose.* Charleston: S. Hart, 1845.

Simms, William Gilmore. *The Letters of William Gilmore Simms,* ed. Mary C. Simms Oliphant, Alfred Taylor Odell, and T. C. Duncan Eaves. 5 vols. Columbia: Univ. of South Carolina Press, 1952-1956.

————. "Our Early Authors and Artists." *XIX Century,* 1 (Sept., 1869), 273-283; 2 (Jan., 1870), 631-637.

[Snowden, Yates]. "South Carolina Plays and Playwrights" in *The Carolinian* (November, 1909).

Sonneck, O. G. *Early Opera in America.* New York: G. Schirmer, 1915.

The South in the Building of the Nation. Richmond: The Southern Historical Publication Society, 1909-1913.

[Taveau, Augustin Louis.] *The Vindication: A Satire, on "Charleston: A Poem."* Charleston: n.p., 1848. (A copy is held by the Univ. of North Carolina Library.)

Taylor, Rosser H. *Ante-Bellum South Carolina: A Social and Cultural History.* Chapel Hill: Univ. of North Carolina Press, 1942.

Three Centuries of Drama: American, ed. Henry W. Wells. New York: Readex Microprint. (See G. William Bergquist for the checklist.)

Trent, William P. *William Gilmore Simms.* Boston: Houghton, Mifflin, 1892.

Wakelyn, Jon L. *The Politics of a Literary Man: William Gilmore Simms.* Westport, Conn.: Greenwood Press, 1973.

Wallace, David Duncan. *South Carolina: A Short History, 1520-1948.* Chapel Hill: Univ. of North Carolina Press, 1951.

Waring, Dr. Joseph Ioor. *A History of Medicine in South Carolina, 1670-1825.* Columbia: S. C. Medical Association, 1964.

Watson, Charles S. "A Denunciation on the Stage of Spanish Rule: James Workman's *Liberty in Louisiana* (1804)." *Louisiana History,* 11 (Summer, 1970), 245-258.

————. "Early Dramatic Writing in the South: Virginia and South Carolina Plays, 1798-1830." Diss. Vanderbilt, 1966. (*Dissertation Abstracts,* 27, no. 10, 3435-A.)

————. "Eighteenth and Nineteenth Century Drama," in *A Bibliographical Guide to the Study of Southern Literature,* ed. Louis D. Rubin, Jr. Baton Rouge: Louisiana State Univ. Press, 1969.

————. "Jeffersonian Republicanism in William Ioor's *Independence,* the First Play of South Carolina." *South Carolina Historical Magazine,* 69 (July, 1968), 194-203.

————. "Stephen Cullen Carpenter: First Drama Critic of the Charleston *Courier."* *South Carolina Historical Magazine,* 69 (Oct., 1968), 243-252.

Webber, Mabel L. "Records from the Blake and White Bibles." *South Carolina Historical and Genealogical Magazine,* 36 (Jan.-Oct., 1935), 14-24, 42-55, 89-93, 113-121; 37 (Jan., April, 1936), 38-44, 65-70.

Wegelin, Oscar. *Early American Plays, 1714-1830.* A compilation of the titles of plays and dramatic poems written by authors born in or residing in North America previous to 1830. New York: The Literary Collector Press, 1905.

White, Edward Brickell. Letter to William Gilmore Simms, dated May 17, 1860. (In possession of the Charles Carroll Simms Collection of the South Caroliniana Library.)

White, John Blake. "Address Delivered at the Medical College. Broad St. at the Request of the Young Men's Temperance Society." August 9,

1836. (In possession of the South Carolina Historical Society.)

————. "An Essay on the Moral Effect and tendency of Capital Punishment, and upon the propriety of substitutiing punishment of a milder nature." July 14, 1834. (In possession of the South Carolina Historical Society.)

————. "An Essay on the Moral Excellence of Painting and shewing the superiority of its powers over those of Poetry." March 9, 1832. (In possession of the South Carolina Historical Society.)

————. "The Journal of John Blake White," ed. Paul R. Weidner. *South Carolina Historical and Geanealogical Magazine,* 42 (April, July, Oct., 1941), 55-71, 99-117, 169-186; 43 (Jan., April, July, 1942), 35-46, 103-117, 161-174.

————. Letter to Richard Henry Dana, Sr., dated Feb. 19, 1844, Charleston. (In possession of the Massachusetts Historical Society.)

————. Letter to "Dana," dated August 16, 1830, Columbia. (In possession of the South Carolina Society.)

————. Letter to Judge R. M. Charlton of Savannah, dated June 21, 1841, Charleston. (In possession of the Historical Society of Pennsylvania.)

————. Letter to John Trumbull, July, 1835. (In possession of the Historical Society of Pennsylvania.)

————. Letter to Joel R. Poinsett, dated March 10, 1837, Charleston. (In possession of the Historical Society of Pennsylvania.)

————. *An Oration . . . in Commemoration of the Adoption of the Federal Constitution.* Charleston: Printed at the Office of the *Southern Patriot,* 1815.

Willis, Eola. *The Charleston Stage in the XVIII Century.* Columbia: The State Co., 1924.

Willis, Eola. Unpublished manuscript dealing with the Placide family now in the possession of the Charleston Free Library.

Wolfe, J. H. *Jeffersonian Democracy in South Carolina.* Chapel Hill: Univ. of North Carolina Press, 1940.

II. Newspapers consulted

Charleston *City Gazette,* 1804-1807; 1818-1824.

Charleston *Courier,* 1803-1859.

Charleston *Times,* 1804-1812.

Richmond *Enquirer,* 1811-1812.

Southern Patriot, 1819.

INDEX

181